Transits of the Planets

Dr. Heber J. Smith

No part of this book may be reproduced or transcribed in any form or by any means, electronic or mechanical, including photocopying or recording or by any information storage and retrieval system without written permission from the publisher, except in the case of brief quotations embodied in critical reviews and articles. Requests and inquiries may be mailed to: American Federation of Astrologers, Inc., 6535 S. Rural Road, Tempe, AZ 85283.

ISBN-10: 0-86690-232-5
ISBN-13: 978-0-86690-232-8

Cover Design: Jack Cipolla

Published by:
American Federation of Astrologers, Inc.
6535 S. Rural Road
Tempe, AZ 85283

www.astrologers.com

Printed in the United States of America

Contents

Transits of the Planet Mercury   1
Transits of the Planet Venus   9
Transits of the Planet Sun   19
Transits of the Planet Mars   29
The Major Planets   33
Transits of the Planet Jupiter   35
Transits of the Planet Saturn   45
Transits of the Planet Uranus   53
Transits of the Planet Neptune   69
Transits   75

Transits of the Planet Mercury

The transits of Mercury are not over-important unless Mercury happens to become retrograde or stationary in important places. Yet the effects are quite marked, and when Mercury adds his influence to that of the other planets, he greatly intensifies their effects. The transits of Mercury, in accord with the law that the transits of the minor planets over the major are identical in quality with the transits of the major over the minor, although differing in degree and duration to the various planets, will affect chiefly the mind and nervous system, and will refer to all matters in which the mind, objectively, is concerned.

In a general sense, the unfavorable transits of Mercury indicate restless, irritating, worrying, and harassing conditions, while the favorable transits indicate mental progress, balance, poise, personal content, mental harmony, right decision, and nervous normality, as well as well-directed action, and successful effort. The evil transits of Mercury are very unfavorable for nervous complaints, irritability, associations with people, and in cases of confirmed mental or nervous pathologic states and will do much to irritate and intensify such states.

Mercury in Aspect to Venus
This is not important, but in the favorable aspects, turns the mind in the direction of art, music, pleasure, gaiety, somewhat stimulates the emotions, and aids to the sociability, and the evil aspects, may do all this, but in a more marked degree.

Mercury in Conjunction, Square, or Opposition to Mars
This aspect tends toward irritability, impulsive speech, and expression and hasty, immature judgment. It is likely, on the one hand, to lead to quarrels, misunderstandings, anger, and the exhibition of some temper, and may lead you to be too critical, impatient and sharp, and too free in the expression of your ideas. People should try to be diplomatic in their relations with others, patient with those who are trying in their behavior, and if they feel out of harmony with others and their conditions, it is likely to be their own fault, while these vibrations often bring criticism, involve one in arguments, disputes, and unfavorable comment, and lead to things that one would have rather left unsaid or undone.

The whole nature of the aspect is toward irritating the nerves and intensifying the mental action, and is apt to bring you in contact with people and conditions that are very irritating and annoying—your correspondence is likely to be troublesome, others are likely to draw out of you expressions of anger and impatience, and your petty affairs are likely to become involved, confused, or worrying. Do nothing precipitate, say nothing that is not well considered, write nothing you are sure will cause offense, and the less you have to do with correspondence, legal affairs, and the operations of the mind at this time, the better. It is a poor time to write important letters, to make decisions of the moment, and for thinking up new ideas.

Mars in Unfavorable Aspect to Mercury
These aspects are similar in effect and are likely to be even more marked, but quite identical in quality.

Mercury in Favorable Aspect to Mars
This aspect is favorable for travel, for mental matters generally, and more especially for those that require forceful expression, accuracy of definition, and that are intended to work some positive results. It is favorable for any form of physical activity, as it lends vigor, strength, and vitality to the muscles. Otherwise, it is not important.

The favorable aspects of the planet Mars to the place of Mercury can be considered similarly, but as being rather more important.

Mercury in Conjunction or Good Aspect to Jupiter
The planet Jupiter has a special bearing upon finance and all constructive, useful, and beneficial operations in the Universe, and is the planet of preservation, of peace and harmony, and has a natural ruling over all things that are in their nature lasting, permanent, and productive of the mental, spiritual, and bodily as well as emotional comfort of the human race. For instance, in the physical world, Jupiter has a great deal to do with finance, which is the physical home and all its accessories. Therefore, the aspects of Mercury to Jupiter produce hopefulness, confidence and faith in oneself, and make the mental action positive, harmonious, and constructive in tune with the minds of others, and therefore disposed to listen to advice, to express diplomatically, tactfully, and moderately, to act maturely, practically and with the very best sense of utility and worth.

All the attributes of the planet Jupiter may be summed up in the word "practical" as it is popularly applied to various human activities. Anything is said to be popularly applied to various human activities. Anything is said to be practical which is found to be productive of positive and appreciable good, and this is what Jupiter implies. This is a good aspect under which to write, to attend to correspondence, legal affairs, and to deal with people through the medium of the mind. Under this influence you are more reasonable, tolerant, kindly, and less nervous, irritated, and impatient than usual, and your mind is likely to be more open, more harmonious, more practical than at other times. This is a good aspect for the spirits, for your dealings and associations with other people, and it is one of the best under which to make important decisions, and especially those that concern your physical and financial well-being and your general status in the world. It is at this time that you will be sensible.

Mercury in Evil Aspect to Jupiter
This aspect is inclined to be too hopeful, too sanguine, too sure, and it is a poor influence under which to make important decisions, attend to important financial and legal affairs, and while it is a very important aspect, it may join its forces with others to make you act unwisely in these things. You are likely to "reckon without your host" and take too much for granted. It tends toward making promises you cannot keep, picturing things more favorable than they really are, and a species of misrepresentation that is not deliberate deceit but which arises from the fact that for the time your impression of things is too highly colored. In all practical matters be, therefore, conservative and do not be too sure of things turning out just as you want them.

Mercury in Conjunction or Evil Aspect to Saturn
This is a depressing influence, and physically, first of all, inclined to nervous troubles and aggravation of such things as neuralgia, rheumatism, and kindred difficulties which might already exist. (not important enough to cause them). You are likely to feel discouraged, unhappy, mentally out of tune, dull, and somewhat pessimistic. Bad for correspondence, and you may receive letters that are unsatisfactory, certain unwelcome news, or fail to receive the letters you are expecting. Be careful what you put in writing, and although you will be skeptical, also be skeptical of your own judgement, and make no important decisions until the aspect has passed. Give your attention to the most routine part of your business life and try to associate with people who are cheerful and optimistic. Try not to be too critical, sarcastic, or otherwise cranky.

Mercury in Good Aspect to Saturn
This influence is good for steady mental work, application and thought, and favors mental dealings with older people. It is slightly favorable for legal affairs, and particularly good for making important decisions in matters that will not mature hastily. It is not a very important aspect but good for concentration, continuity, and deep thought.

Mercury in Conjunction or Evil Aspect to Uranus
These conditions are excitable, irritating, nervous, and tense. You may be inclined to be sarcastic, impatient, irritable, and very uncertain. Try and be diplomatic in your dealings with others, and skeptical of your judgement. The tendency is to be impatient with forms, customs, and accepted ideas, to want to think along new lines, and try mental experiments. It is very unfavorable for applications, routine work, and a time when you may find it exceedingly difficult to stay by your usual work, accustomed opinions, and maintain a steady line of conduct.

This aspect is highly nervous and irritating to the mind, which is inclined to search for new ideas and to be dissatisfied with its usual routine. You are very apt to have trouble with those with whom you are generally associating, as being under such intense vibrations you are apt to behave in an unaccountably restless, cranky manner, to be subject to changes of opinion and intention can be rather unreliable. It is a bad time to make important decisions, and in case of the evil aspects, decidedly bad for correspondence and writing, or for dealing with people on the mental plane. You may be inclined to entertain unpopular views, indulge in eccentric forms of expression, and generally antagonize people, while in the case of the conjunction, if there are any good aspects to the planet Uranus radically or by direction, you may receive new ideas that will be worth considering and be mentally active and keen.

All the aspects mentioned are apt to bring sudden and unexpected meetings with people, look for news or events mainly of a trifling nature. However, as the general influence of the planet Uranus is rather explosive and productive at all times unexpected things are apt to go queerly, matters become tangled and confused, and cause a certain amount of worry and petty annoyance, and your minor affairs are likely to "pile up" on you, and cause you to be worried, hurried, and otherwise tied up in knots.

Do not lay too much stress upon the simple transits of one of Mercury's positions over that of Uranus, as that will not be very marked, but both Mercury's transit at the same time, say one square and other conjunction to Uranus, radical place or Mercury pass over that body in company with the Sun or Mars, the worry, confusion, and general tendency to confuse, disarrange, and hurry will be rather marked. Always take into account the other aspects that may be made at the same time, as well as the radical or progressed positions of the planet which the transiting body might meet at the same time, as all of these influences will be very modifying. For instance, if the Sun and Mercury transited the conjunction of Uranus and Mars was square Uranus at birth, the influence would be, of course, very potent, but should Uranus be trine to Jupiter and sextile to Saturn so that Mercury and the Sun made their good aspects at the same time as he made the conjunction to Uranus, then these favorable angles would in a great measure prevent the confusion and enable the person to control the situation to a great degree. Take everything into account, and of course, the chief difficulty lies in the fact that at any given time, there are so many elements to consider that it is very difficult to give a right judgement, but unless in the aggregated influences are decidedly unfavorable, it is useless to expect much trouble, and the contrary.

Mercury in Favorable Aspect or Conjunction to Uranus
If Uranus be well aspected, this is favorable for travel, for thinking up new ideas, for correspondence, for speaking or writing, for publicity, for any mental work, and this is a good time in which to exercise the mind to its fullest capacity. Ideas that come to you at this time are likely to be of some value and while the aspect does not of

itself favor financial affairs, practical, or conservative departments of life, it is splendid for inventions, progress, or ideas out of the ordinary. A good aspect under which to lecture, to meet interesting people of a mental nature, and if you have any important matters to attend to which require your brightest mental efforts, this is a good time to choose. Indicates quick action, rapid, and accurate work, and keen intuition.

Mercury in Conjunction or Evil Aspect to Neptune
This is a queer influence and not all reliable. Look out for deceit, humbug and quacks in general, deceptive ideas, lies, fraud, and do not trust your judgements or other's candor. When Neptune is afflicted, look out for treachery, underhand enmity, scandal, and be careful what you say, sign, or put in writing. Make no important decisions, think up no important ideas and consider the influence generally untrustworthy. It is a "woozy" aspect.

Mercury in Good Aspect or Conjunction to Neptune
Where Neptune is well aspected, this brings unusual ideas, sometimes, and is inspirational and psychic. You may meet peculiar people, especially of a spiritual or psychic type, and you may either receive or express unusual views. It is a subtle influence, leads to intuition, aids music, poetry and the arts, and in many cases, where Neptune is not prominent, it may pass without any appreciable influences. Where Neptune is powerful, it tends to be strong and is associated with unusual impressions, mental illumination, and interesting experiences. Do not expect much, if anything, unless other influences combine. In a general sense the unfavorable transits of Mercury tend to bring unsatisfactory news, unfavorable criticism, lies, deceit, treachery and worry, petty quarreling and disputes, uneven mental action, impaired memory, want of application, interfering influences, and where Mercury makes transits over very much afflicted points, expect unkindness, unpleasant experiences with people, verbal and written attacks, severe criticism, scandal, and the like.

Transits of the Planet Venus

Venus in Favorable Aspect to the Sun
This is very favorable for social affairs, for dealing in a social way with men and for pleasure and friendship, and indicates a good time to plan everything of a social or artistic nature.

Venus in Favorable Aspect to Mercury
These aspects are good for the expression of the artistic faculties, for social amenities, for pleasant correspondence, for associations with people generally, and for one's personal happiness and contentment.

Venus in Favorable Aspects to the Moon
These aspects are fortunate for dealing with women and men, the wife or mother, for domestic affairs, for personal happiness and spirits, for pleasure, travel, and health. It is a fortunate influence under which to interview women, to ask favors of them, and for dealing with the general public, and especially in an artistic or musical way, or where one's personality counts. The conjunction of Venus with the Moon always brings very pleasant experiences through some woman, unless the Moon is vilely afflicted and tends

to the expression of the emotional nature, to indulgence, sensuality, and physical enjoyment, especially where the Moon is in such signs as Taurus, Cancer, Scorpio, and Capricorn.

Venus Aspects to Mars
This stirs up the emotional nature very strongly and tends to impulsive expression of the affections, sudden attacks of love, and, sometimes, lovers quarrels that are likely to end in petty displays of emotion, and charming relapses into delightful mushiness. It is a very good aspect under which to "raise the devil" with your inamorata in the hopes of getting things going. In a more serious vein, the sexual instincts need guarding under the aspect, and where there is plentiful interchange of these two planets at any time in a horoscope, whether by transit of Venus to Mars or the reverse, radical or progressed, the mind is inclined to seek affection, sympathy and love, and the person is in the mood for enjoyment. In the favorable aspects, there is plenty of magnetism, activity but less likelihood of folly, and more of satisfaction, and in the adverse aspects there is the tendency to force conditions, be very impatient, passionate, and foolhardy and things are not likely to go as smoothly or satisfactorily.

Venus in Conjunction or Good Aspect to Jupiter
This is one of the more fortunate minor transits. First of all it is favorable for artistic and social matters, a good influence under which to meet people, make friends, entertain, or be entertained. Next it usually brings favors, kindness and gifts, and usually fortunate for financial affairs in general; money usually comes more easily than usual under this aspect.

Jupiter governs the most conventional and conservative, as well as the most permanent departments of life, and has a natural long standing, so this influence is a very favorable one under which to visit relatives, the home, parents, or old friends. One usually sees old friends at this time and sometimes meets them unexpectedly. It is exceedingly happy in its influence, and all matters of pleasures and enjoyment are sure to go rightly under this aspect. If you want to entertain, give a concert, or display work of an artistic nature, this is a good time to choose, and anything of this nature is sure to be satisfactory at this time. It is a good time in which to repair quarrels, patch up friendships, or renew acquaintance, and you are pretty sure to get good treatment at the hands of others at this time.

It encourages generosity, tends to expenditures, assists extravagance, makes one more careful of their dress and deportment, and while expansive in nature it is all in the direction and along the lines of conservation. It is a good aspect under which to seek the friendship of the wealthy, and distinguished in society, and those in superior positions. It is favorable for any matters connected with the home, the family, or the financial standing, and owing to the fact that under this aspect the financial and social are blended harmoniously, it is pretty good for anything and everything in the common run of things.

Venus in Evil Aspect to Jupiter
This is, par excellence, the aspect of social boredom. The influence of this aspect is to place you amid circumstances which are trying from the fact of their being formal, too conservative, too stiff and elegant for comfort, and with people who are too conventional, who are perhaps expensively dressed and appointed, richly caparisoned, so to speak but very uninteresting and it tends to put you where you are dissatisfied, more or less chocked and hampered with too much ceremony and rich surroundings and it is inclined to lead to extravagance, display, and ostentation and the feeling is apt to be that it was not all worthwhile.

It is a poor aspect under which to plan entertainments as they are likely to be more expensive than edifying, and for being entertained, as you are likely to wish yourself somewhere else. In case this sort of thing suits you, you are fortunate for this particular time, even if unfortunate when not so conditioned, but I have always found the evil aspects of Venus to Jupiter very annoying, barren, uninteresting, and disgustingly decent. It is not an important influence because it brings nothing positively favorable, and is neither good for finance nor for anything else, and the only good thing about it is that it is good discipline for the disposition as it puts you where you have to behave where you would not dare to say one rotten word. It indicates fat ladies, well-fitted dining tables, gilded cages, and vapidly pleasant social intercourse, in which there will not be one word of real sense, or genuine feeling. On the other hand, while it inclines to decorum and engenders perfect deportment, you will be so horrified at the realization of the ideal that you will probably swear never to be respectable again. It enforces correct costuming, and prompt replies to invitations, as well as rapid acknowledgment of favors received. In fact, it is a holy horror! Perhaps the best feature of this trying situation is that it does not last long, unless Venus is retrograde, in which case it is best to go to bed until it is over.

People you meet under this aspect are likely to be optimistic and well nourished, have a great regard for the etiquette column in the Sunday paper and their idea of being devilish is only going to church three times on Sunday and if possible four. Their equatorial circumference is likely to exceed their polar diameter by more than the aesthetic standard requires. They are likely to welcome you with a fat smile, and be very much over-bolstered. In case Jupiter is radically afflicted, the type is not so pure, which makes one willing to put up with that calamity if for no other reason. For further particulars, refer to the *The Book of Snobs* written by one, Thackeray.

Venus in Good Aspect or Conjunction to Uranus
We are now able to breathe again. These are very magnetic vibrations, but very capricious. The unexpected is likely to happen in your social affairs. You may meet someone unexpectedly, make a new acquaintance; and the unconventional side of your nature will be to the front. It is a very interested time in which to plan social affairs, meetings, and pleasures generally, and whatever takes place

under these vibrations is sure to be diverting—thank God. This is a good aspect for artistic affairs, which are sure to be artistic successes, even if not financially so, which especially belongs to Jupiter, and it is a very active inspiring agent. If you want things to be very brilliant and interesting, this is the aspect for which to plan and especially if the contemplated function is in the least Bohemian.

In case Uranus is afflicted at birth, the conjunction inclines rather too much, to unconventionality, and may provoke you to be a little indiscreet or regardless of conventions, which would be a lamentable thing. On the other hand, people you meet under this aspect (conjunction) will be interesting characters, magnetic, and fascinating, but in the case of the afflicted Uranus, unreliable, and if you put too much stock in them, you will be disappointed. The best way is to expect nothing of them, enjoy them while they last, which will not be long, and when they disappear magically, do not be disappointed. In the case of the favorable aspect, they are not so selfish and you may possible see them again.

Venus in Evil Aspect to Uranus
This is a very unconventional and erratic influence. Your emotions are very active, and you may feel disposed to act without the advice of Mrs. Gundy. You may meet someone very interesting, but do not take them seriously, as the influence is capricious, and while you might seem to be getting along famously, it is likely to come to nothing in the end. The unexpected, sudden, and unlooked for is likely to happen, and it is best not to plan too rigidly for this aspect, as your plans are likely not to come to pass. Be a little guarded in the expression of your emotional nature, and if you take chances, be a sport, and do not wail if you have to pay the price. This aspect never brings anything permanent or satisfactory, but it is often provocative of alluring overtures and enticing promises. Try and be guided by reason and sound judgement, and do not let your feelings run away with you.

Venus in Conjunction or Evil Aspect to Saturn
This is decidedly a nasty one. Plan nothing social for this time. You are likely to expect too much of your friends and you may feel somewhat dull, unhappy or slighted, and get your precious feelings hurt. If you are disposed to be jealous, now is the time for the exhibition of this charming trait, and misunderstandings, grouchiness, sensitivity, wounded feelings, and tragedies constructed out of vague imaginings and slights will not be so nice to you at this time, so be a sport and smile if it kills you.

Your plans for pleasure are apt to go wrong, if it is only the whether. The one person you wanted to see will not turn up, the company will be dull and stupid, the arrangements poor, and the dinner beastly. The person you sit next to will be unattractive, your hair will not curl, your nose will be shiny and your hose holey. You will look your worst, behave your worst, and have the satisfaction of realizing that you look at least forty years older than you are. You will act awkwardly, say yes when you mean no, and be studiously misunderstood. The friend you counted on will spend his smiles somewhere else, your rival will have a more fascinating frock and look indecently ravishing, you will not get the largest piece of pie, and you will have an extra bad attack of disjointed proboscis. You will not be the center of attraction, your smile will not dazzle as of old, and every mirror you gaze in will insult you unmercifully. It is a good time to stay home and mend the family linen.

It is a propitious time for washing the week's dishes and dusting the family Bible. And its dollars to doughnuts that all the ladies you call on will not be at home, and especially the one whom you always call "dear," the line will be busy when you want to talk to your twin sister, who, as you know, has just the most interesting something to tell you. Mr. Z, who is so clever and interesting, and understands you so well, will not be at Mrs. A's this afternoon to tea, so it is no use your going, and if you do not go, why of course, he will be there. Mr. B, by the way, thinks she understands him as no other woman in the world ever could or did—the hussy. In short, and not to go through any further detail, it is a maddening influence, and the less you expect, the better.

The best thing to do, as I have hinted, is to stay home, have a good shampoo, dig out the corners of the parlor floor, and mend your husband's socks. It is bad for social affairs, music, art of anything in the nature of sentiment, love or pleasure or gaiety, and unless there are very powerful contrary aspects, you may as well expect the worst.

Venus in Good Aspect to Saturn
This is a very negative aspect, and conduce your good behavior, discretion, and the association of older people, self-control, and all thee dull proceedings. It is a very meaningless aspect, and does not seem to bring much of anything, and probably, like most of the favorable aspects of Saturn, is more restrictive and controlling in effect than anything else. Venus and Saturn both negative in nature, nothing happens. On the other hand, it can act as a preventive in case of too much hilarity, a disposition to be kittenish or unquiet emotional states, and where this aspect exists, there is not likely to be any indiscretion. Saturn conceals, and governs things through prudence, reason, and caution, and it is therefore a good aspect when considered as an offset to Mars and Uranus.

Venus in Evil Aspect to Neptune
This is a misleading influence that tends to peculiar emotional states and psychic influences. People you meet under this aspect are likely to exercise a very subtle influence over you and charm you in some way which is not superficial. It is, however, a rather treacherous influence and not be relied upon. Act on this influence and you are apt to wish you had not and one of the most common effects of it is to make you think you are in love when you are not, or make you think that someone else cares for you when they do not. It implies self-deception, sometimes, and people under this stimulus are apt to let their emotions lead them too much.

If Neptune is well aspected, in the case of the conjunction, it may indicate at time a very subtle, in the case of the conjunction, it may indicate at times a very subtle, spiritual, and elevating influence, and in any case, always a fascinating one. But the thing is not to be taken in and not to pay too much attention to, or be guided by your feelings under this aspect. Wait till other aspects set in and see how you feel then. If the accompanying aspects were good and Neptune, as aforesaid, well aspected, then the conjunction sometimes indicates a very strong and profound influence.

I have an intimate friend, and on the day we met, Venus was transiting his Neptune by conjunction, Neptune being well aspected to the Sun, Mercury, Jupiter, and Uranus. He told me that on the day he met me he knew that we would be very great friends, and he plainly felt a very powerful influence at work. He has Neptune rising and is very psychic. We are enjoying an unusual and close friendship in which the mutual relationship has been most beneficial. But as a general rule it is a misleading influence and needs careful watching, and in many cases, probably has no results. There is usually something odd about either the person or the process of the meeting, and in this case, the circumstances leading up to our meeting were decidedly peculiar.

Venus in Unfavorable Aspect to Neptune
This is apt to be decidedly unconventional, and with a touch of the romantic, the strange, or the mysterious. It is not to be trusted, leads to unwise expression of the emotional nature, and there is sure to be an atmosphere of deceit, double-dealing, masquerading, or something of the kind. Do not trust people you meet where this is the dominant note at the time as they are misrepresenting themselves, or you are deceiving yourself about them. Your sympathies are likely to be aroused, and you are likely to be motivated by pity, compassion, or some subtle psychic force which bodes no good.

Of course, where this aspect happens to be a dominant note at the time, it is best to beware. When I say the dominant note, this would be the case, for instance, where the Sun, Mercury, or Mars was transiting at the same time, or where there was some important direction, especially to Venus, Mercury, or Neptune in the progressed horoscope, and more than one transit at the same time, or where one position of Venus was transiting Neptune and the other Uranus, or its evil aspect, or some such mix-up. where the other aspects are very normal, then Neptune will do not more than throw an air or mystery around things, or romance, and adds slightly to the flavor of the unusual, which must be just enough to make the combination interesting.

Never look for marked effects unless there is some sort of concerted effect, for although I have tried to describe these aspects very carefully, and give them the right coloring, I have exaggerated in order to do so, and if they all work out just as I have said, life would be too interesting to ever leave. The whole difficulty lie in the correct analysis of mixtures, and giving things their right proportions.

Transits of the Planet Sun

Sun in Evil Aspect or Conjunction to Saturn
The periods when the Sun makes the conjunction or evil aspect of Saturn mark the most depressing times of the year, and especially for health and general business affairs. This is a very unfavorable time for any work of an initiative nature, and is only fit for working on matters already under way. It slows up the functions generally, causes one to be most susceptible to colds or any trouble which is the result of poor elimination, and one should avoid at this time getting overheated and cooling off too quickly. One is apt to feel very tired, dragged, and somewhat lacking in "snap," if nothing more.

Sun in Evil Aspect or Conjunction to Uranus
This transit causes one to feel much stirred up and very intense, and it is a time when it takes little to throw you off your poise. In the case of the conjunction and where Uranus has evil aspects in the radix to Mercury, the Moon or Mars, it is a very disturbed time indeed, and when everything is apt to go awry for a few days. If subject to nervous trouble, this aspect will intensify them or bring them out. Be very skeptical of all propositions made to you at this time, and if you have any new ideas of a radical nature for conduct-

ing your business or life at this be cautious about putting them into execution, and it will be better to wait and see if, after the passage of this transit, they will still seem to you as practical, or attractive as they did. If you feel totally out of harmony, dissatisfied with your condition, and with the people about you, restless, nervous, and on edge, be patient, as it is a condition that will soon pass off. This aspect is apt to bring the element of the unexpected into the life and events of a sudden and unlooked for nature are apt to happen. If you have any important matters under way, do not be surprised if they suddenly fall through at the last moment, as it is the very nature of Uranus to bring disaster at the last moment.

Sun in Good Aspect to Uranus
(including quintile and sesquiquintile, 108 degrees)
This is a very favorable condition for having dealings with corporations, the government, and large enterprises out of the ordinary, and it is well to make the most of opportunities which lead up to you at this time. It is favorable for any work of an initiative character, inventing, untried enterprises, or asking favors of people of intellect, genius, attainment, or power, and in general sense, for anything of an unusual type. This transit brightens up the intuition, adds vim and snap to the activities, tones up the system, and is an excellent aspect under which to plan anything which needs special effort, and in the doing of which one needs all of one's inspiration and nervous force.

Sun in Favorable Aspect to Saturn
This is not at all important in respect of the fact that Saturn is a restricting and negative force, and there is not likely to bring about any particular marked event of effect. It is an aspect of self-control, conservatism, caution, and during the operation of which one has oneself in hand more or less and its influence will serve to tone down the effect of any Martial or Uranian aspect which might for the time be in force. It would be a favorable time for seeking favors from old people, for listening to advice, for attending to precautionary measures, and favorable for routine work, finishing up

work that has been already begun, or attending to matters which are by their nature slow, heavy, and monotonous. Favorable for matters which are by their nature connected with the earth, real estate, or old conditions. Whatever good this aspect brings will be on account of its tendency toward control, moderation, and caution, and by process of elimination rather than initiation of the opposite.

Sun in Evil Aspect or Conjunction to Neptune

This is a very unreliable influence, and in all cases, except those where Neptune is a very utilized force, it is best to be skeptical of the people one meets at this time, any propositions made to you, and there is likely to be an element of fraud playing about you during its continuance. Your own ideas are likely to be impractical and unreliable, and singed with some emotional or altruistic streak which may be very pleasant to experience and very dangerous to take too seriously.

In the case of the conjunction, however, where Neptune has favorable aspects in the radix, it might be well to attend to any ideas which come to you at this time, as in this case they are likely not only to be actuated by motives of a very high order, but also capable of fit and successful expression. In other cases, if at this time you feel peculiarly nervous, ill at ease, and depleted or depressed, try to get away from your accustomed surroundings, and from the people with whom you are normally most intimate, as there is something in your mutual magnetism that needs adjusting, and you are probably being unfavorably acted upon on the psychic plane. A brief change of surroundings and associations will be the best possible thing for you. At this time you are likely to be appealed to through your sympathies, and any propositions made to you under these vibrations are likely to be "bubble schemes," or an attempt, however laudable, to get something for nothing by appealing to the higher vibrations in you, so keep your eyes open, and carefully investigate any plans put before you, or any suggestions to reap a quick harvest, they will usually be either impracticable, founded on crazy ideas, or else deceptive, visionary, or otherwise unsatisfactory, and above all, see that the person is not trying to pull the wool over your eyes.

Sun in Favorable Aspect to Neptune
A very subtle vibration and probably apprehended by very few individuals, and not of very great importance unless the horoscope shows Neptune to be active and vital. In this case it usually brings to bear aspiration of a very spiritual and transcendental order, throwing into activity the altruistic, devotional, unselfish, and serving elements of the character, inspiring one to act of kindness, charity, love of one's king, etc., and it is the most favorable time for experience of a high order, whether purely psychic or emotional. Under the vibrations, one may experience ennobling sentiments, and undergo spiritual or religious phases but it all depends on the condition of the horoscope; and in a great many cases the more delicate and subtle essence of Neptune is quite lost among the coarser vibrations of Mars, Jupiter, and Saturn. In practical ways, little can be said of it. Neptune works mainly on the psychic plane' but it would at least be well not to disregard any unusual influence which might enter the life at this time as it would be likely to be of some importance spiritually, and meant for one's higher development; and it is under aspects of this sort that inner experiences come.

Sun in Favorable Aspect to Jupiter
Just as Saturn marks off the most unfavorable periods of the life, and the Sun's transits to him, the most troublesome periods of the year; so the Sun's aspects to Jupiter point out the most favorable periods of the year from the material and general standpoint. These vibrations are magnetic, health giving, toning up the system; giving courage through confidence, faith, hope, ambition, strength, and power; from the wealthy, from one's friends or relations and particularly the male sex, and at this time one naturally approaches people in such a manner as to stir the best in them. When one has confidence, one naturally inspires confidence. Accordingly, almost anything of a reasonable nature that one undertakes at this

time will go through at this time satisfactorily; and it is an exceedingly good time for work of a constructive and an initiatory nature and if you have any important financial matters to attend to, this is the best time in which to do so. Do not reject any propositions made to you at this time, and any people you may meet, so long as it is not in a purely social way, are likely to be friendly to you and favor your cause. Anything you commence at this time should go forward fairly well, and any plans or propositions that come up to you are likely to prove important and beneficial, even if at first they may not appear so, this aspect is favorable for health and favorable for one's dealing with the male sex, as well as for the members of the family.

In all respects, the periods covered by the Sun's aspects to Jupiter will be the most fortunate and beneficial of the year, unless it should happen that the Sun forms at the same period the very evil aspects of the malefics; which will hardly happen at every transit; although it might start some of them especially where Jupiter is heavily afflicted and when the Sun's conjunction will not bring the benefit that it should.

Sun in Evil Aspect to Jupiter
This cannot be considered a very evil aspect as it is not at all depressing or unhappy in its influence. Far to the contrary, it is a very hopeful, confident, and sanguine influence, but can be too much so, and in this lies the evil for it inspires people to be too confident, too hopeful, too sure, and to think that there is safety where there is really danger. It is therefore a treacherous influence financially, although not indicating a severe loss; but nothing at this time is likely to turn out satisfactorily or according to one's wishes, it is a transit under which one's expectations are likely to be disappointed through being too expensive.

It is best not to trust people who bring you propositions at this time as they are likely to be impractical or misrepresented. The prospects may read well, but there may be very little at the back of it.

People at this time are likely to allay your fears, hold out promises, and raise your hopes, but if they do so, be on your guard, so the aspect promises little. It is a poor time for an initiative work, and especially where money in involved, and it is likely to lead to eventual loss. It is a poor time for law and for legal affairs and in the case of the square or the opposition, where Jupiter is afflicted by Mercury at birth, it is indicative of litigation, endless worry and vexation, red tape, form, ceremony observance, and all the time killers that can be thrown in the way of the unwary. It is a safe rule not to allow oneself to be drawn into any financial or legal affairs at this time, and to be most cautious where money is involved. If Jupiter is afflicted at birth by Uranus, Saturn, or Mars, it is a time when serious loss may take place.

On the personal side, this aspect means enthusiasm, unwise impulse, the tendency to make greater promises than one can fulfill and in a general way, a to great expansion of the feelings that may result in foolish expenditure, indiscreet generosity, and in some cases religious mania or excitation. In a word, one should avoid at this time allowing one's self to be carried away by one's feelings, hopes, or ambitions and expectations, which in this case, are likely to be unreliable and misleading.

Sun in Aspect to Venus
There are several aspects of minor import whose results are similar. Sometimes several of them come at the same time. These are: good or bad aspects of Sun to Venus, Venus to Sun, Mars to Venus, and Venus to Mars.

All these have the effect of raising the emotional or sex nature, and making one more susceptible to beauty, music, art, the attractions of the opposite sex, amusement, pleasure, love of dress and finery, and making one more magnetic; and in the case of the favorable aspects, especially of Venus to the Sun and the Sun to Venus, it is a good time for planning social affairs, amusements, and for pleasures generally, or for arranging meetings with those for whom you care and with whom you wish to enjoy yourself. The evil aspects have all the effect of making one magnetic and putting one in the right mood for enjoying, but under their influence things are not likely to go so smoothly, or to one's satisfaction, and one may be inclined to force issues, strain the natural order of circumstances in order to gain a point, or in some way to act foolishly and unadvisedly.

The transits of the Sun to the places of Venus, geo and helio, radical and progressed are worth watching, for under the conjunction or even the trine or sextile, one sometimes meets people who play an important part in life; but if there are no important transits of the major planets operating on Venus at the time, and particularly of Uranus and Jupiter, nothing of note need be expected. However, very pleasant influences are always brought about by the Sun to the conjunction, sextile, trine Venus; Venus conjunction, trine, sextile Sun; and even Venus aspecting her own place by good aspects, while the aspects of Venus to Mars and the contrary, when good, increases the magnetism, promotes gaiety and lively amusement; and in the unfavorable aspects act very strangely on the emotional nature, and incline to indiscretion and dangerous impulses.

As a general rule, do not plan social matters, meetings with friends, and all things which concern pleasure, art, music, etc., on the bad aspects more than you can help and the more favorable aspects that you can find to the places of Venus, whether from the Sun, Mars, Venus, or Mercury or those to Venus to Mercury and the Sun, and the Moon transiting a favorable aspect only concern things of a transitory nature, the really important things and lasting affairs come under the major transits.

Sun in Evil Aspect to Mars, Mars in Evil Aspect to Sun
Mars here gives force and energy to the feelings. The native is inclined to adopt a too dictatorial attitude, to act on impulse, and to use force, to try to try things through regardless of the feelings of

others, and as a result, quarrels, misunderstandings, and even violence may result, according to the horoscope. The thing to do is to try to keep harmony at this time, to use patience and discretion, to avoid forcing issues, and whatever might be attempted at this time is likely to be founded upon impulses that are misleading. Conditions of unpleasantness, of great intensity are sometime bought about through the transit of Mars to the Sun, but owing to the transient nature of that planet, they are short lived, and nothing should be done, no great alterations made, and no issue taken on this aspect—it always tends to cause people to do things for which they are sorry, very soon after; and as soon as the Martial aspect disappears, they are apt to find that they had no good safe or sane reason for acting.

Mars in Unfavorable Aspect to the Sun
This is an indication of quarrels, differences and misunderstandings with the male sex, and in the nativities of married women difficulties with the husband, or in others, with the father, lover, or any male intimate in the life. it also indicates danger of accident, sometimes, and especially when making the transit while Uranus or Saturn are afflicting the Sun by transit at the same time. This planet in transit also is likely to bring about sudden attacks of illness of an inflammatory sort to aggravate evil conditions already prevailing, and while positive and vitalizing in its nature, it may result in those forms of ill health that are caused by fever, overacting, excitement, overheating, and the like.

Never judge a transit of Mars as either dangerous or lasting unless either Saturn, Jupiter, or Uranus are all in aspect at the same time of the transit; as in the case of Roosevelt who had Uranus squaring the Sun and the helio Mars in conjunction the day he was shot. If Uranus had not been in aspect too, Mars would never have caused it. Roosevelt had also a progressed secondary direction of mars to conjunct helio Saturn radical on the Ascendant in Leo, very near square of the radical Sun at the time—according to the *Nautical Almanac*) Mars transits the Sun two or three times a year, and it is only when some ponderable body assists, that danger really threatens. The other possible case is where, for instance, the radical Sun is afflicted by Mars, on the progressed horoscope by other planets; as events are caused 1) by violent concerted attack of planetary aspects to one point of the horoscope, and 2) by attack of several planets in transit to several points of the horoscope, whether by direction or radix, that indicates a similarity of effect—as, for instance, where the radical Sun might have the conjunction of Mars radically, and the progressed Sun the square of Uranus radically; and where both points were afflicted in transit by Mars, the Sun, and either Jupiter, Uranus, or Saturn, and especially the last two. The main point at issue being that the simple transit of the Sun to Mars is similar in nature, but not as marked in effect. The radical place of Mars is not a vital point, though it is an afflicted one.

Sun in Good Aspect to Mars, Mars in Good Aspect to Sun
This is not so important, and simply indicates the time when the vital forces are active, a good time for enterprises, health, and pushing through those things that require courage, energy, and initiative. It distinctly favors health and is a favorable period for the adoption of forceful or drastic measures, for operations, or for any form of force. It is a good foil for the evil influences of Saturn. It is neither so powerful, so lasting or beneficial as Jupiter, but it is a force of a similar sort, but more active, assertive, and indicates activity and particularly physical activity.

Sun in Aspect to Mercury, Mercury in Aspect to Sun
This is not of importance, but if Mercury is afflicted at birth, it then becomes very important, and the nature of the influence will be in accordance with the particular aspect. It, of course, vitalizes and intensifies the mental action, and in the case where Mercury is fairly well conditioned, it gives force, energy, and activity to the mind. It is then good for correspondence, for planning, ideas, for all matters which concern papers and documents and legal affairs, but this will only be where Mercury is well supported, the very contrary being the case where it is not.

Sun in Evil Aspect to Mercury
This is a worrying, fretful, restless, and nervous aspect, tending toward change, movement, uncertainty and confusion, and more especially of course, where Mercury is afflicted by Mars, Uranus, or the Moon. Events are likely to become chaotic at this time, and matters mixed and tangled, with consequent indecision, hurry, confusion, and strain. It is best not to make important decisions under this aspect, unless there are favorable aspects of Mercury at the same time, or unless the place of Mercury is very well aspected.

In a general sense, the Sun brings things to pass, although it is not the only influence which does so, but this much will be true; the sun seems more or less, to concentrate the forces in the direction of his transits; that is to say, if matters of a more or less Martial character are under way, the transit of the Sun over Mars will precipitate things, and the same of any other. The transit of the Sun to afflicted points of the horoscope are very evil times, and it takes very powerful and positive aspects otherwise to mitigate the effects.

If you have some particular or important matters pending, and it has to culminate at a time when the Sun is square to your Saturn, it is a very evil omen; whereas if it culminates at a time when the Sun is trining your Jupiter, it is equally good. It is not a good idea to commence things when the Sun is aspecting the malefics in your horoscope, and it is good to commence matters when the Sun has the favorable aspects of the benefics; or the favorable aspects of the malefics according to the nature of the matter. The transits of the Sun are very important, and very vital, which can be readily learned from the fact that the transits of the sun over Saturn depresses everybody, devitalizes, and brings things to a momentary standstill; whereas the transit of the Sun is transiting the favorable aspects of Jupiter, everything goes well, unless at this particular aspect, the Sun meets the evil aspects of Saturn or Uranus, or a number of minor impediments. But, of the minor aspects, the Sun's are the most vital and important.

Transits of the Planet Mars

Mars in Conjunction or Evil Aspect to Moon
This stirs up the emotions and the senses, and in horoscopes that are controlled may lead to excesses, petty violence, displays of temper and domestic brawls. it usually indicates trouble with or through women. You may be worried on account of some women intimate in your life, or your domestic affairs may be unsettled and troublesome. You may have trouble with some woman, and at this time, it is necessary to exercise self-control and caution so as not to do so. Annoyances with or through women is the commonest concomitant of this aspect. It also can indicate some trouble with your health, and if the Moon is afflicted at birth it is likely to cause feverish complaints, functional troubles, or slight accidents. You are likely to be excited or angry, and it sometimes causes a journey or makes you want to travel.

Mars in Favorable Aspect to the Moon
This is not at all important.

Mars in Conjunction, Square, or opposition to His Own Place
This usually stirs up the energies, and under this aspect self-control, diplomacy, and caution are needed. Where Mars is afflicted at

birth, slight accidents are possible, especially where Mars afflicts Mercury, when trivial mishaps may occur through carelessness or recklessness. Where Mars afflicts the Sun at birth, it sometimes causes slight cuts, abrasions, or fevers. If Mars, at birth, is afflicted by Saturn or Uranus, then these times may bring accidents, but not as a rule, unless some other planet is transiting the evil aspect of the radical Mars, Saturn, or Uranus at the same time.

Mars in Conjunction or Evil aspect to Jupiter
This is an aspect of impulse, expansion of the feelings, generosity, carelessness, and recklessness in the matter of expenditure in finance. It indicates heavy expense, unsatisfactory purchases, extravagance, loss, theft, and the inclination to take financial risk. It is the typical aspect of loss. Under this aspect, make no important purchases or you will find that you have not acquired what you really wanted, the article is not satisfactory, you have paid too much for it, or you have bought under impulse something you could very well have done without.

Do not be careless about property as you may lose it or be without. Do not be careless about property as you may lose it or be robbed. Hold fast to your pocketbook. Do not speculate or take chances where money is concerned. In a general way, and outside of the financial considerations, which is the most important in the case of this aspect, do not be guided by your feelings, do not be to generous, too magnanimous, and avoid fanaticism, the over-expression of your sentiments, dogmatism. It is also an aspect typical of religious mania, so do not trust any sudden impulse to do quixotic or generous things, or make rash promises or you might find out that you have made a serious mistake, promised more than you can possible perform, or otherwise committed yourself unwisely. Avoid legal matters; you will probably lose.

Mars in Good Aspect to Jupiter
The favorable aspects of Mars to Jupiter tend to act in generosity, courage, and heroism, to deeds which are prompted by nobility,

high sense of duty, manliness, and magnanimity; to large-handedness, to the free expression of the religious instincts, to proselytizing, to hospitality, kindness, and tolerance towards enemies, and to all the deeds which befit the attitude of the strong and the able towards the weak and defenseless. It gives rise to any and every species of action which one naturally identifies with the true nobleman. It tends toward expenditure, but not toward loss.

Mars in Conjunction or Evil Aspect to Saturn
This is an aspect of great inharmony, and one is likely to feel bitter, abused, or badly treated without due cause. It is apt to make things difficult, and for the time being your work may not go right, you may be subjected to treachery or jealousy, and you should be very careful not to place yourself in accidental situations. The temper under this aspect is a little fractious and troublesome, and the tendency to be revengeful and to brood over wrongs more marked.

Mars in Conjunction or Evil Aspect to Uranus
This makes one feel disagreeable, and unless one exercises self-control, the temper is likely to be troublesome and vicious, and antagonism is easily aroused. Accidents sometimes happen, and one's work is likely to go wrong, one is apt to feel reckless, act on very hasty impulse, and to take chances in a rather wild way. The utmost caution is always needed under this aspect.

Mars in Conjunction or Evil Aspect to Neptune
This arouses the emotional nature and is apt to attract peculiar conditions. Where Neptune is afflicted at birth by the Moon or Venus, the sense nature is much stimulated and the imagination very active. There may be a tendency to self-gratification, danger of indulging in drugs or narcotics, and states of great excitability. If Mercury aspects Neptune at birth, this transit is rather hysterical and very emotional, and it is hard to keep to one's work and follow a settled course. The temper is strange, easily aroused, and quickly dispersed.

The Major Planets

The major transits are the most important element in the science of prediction, and everything that can happen to the human being is determined, mainly by these. The critical times in the period of transit will be those times when the Sun and Mars swing also into aspect with the superiors; as for instance, when the transit of Mars afflicts the body that is at the same time afflicted by Saturn and Uranus; these are very marked and very threatening. Even Jupiter in the evil aspects is dangerous in much afflicted nativities; and the combined transit of Saturn and afflicting Jupiter, or of Uranus and afflicting Jupiter, over heavily afflicted points in the nativity must be regarded with caution and suspicion.

It is very important that one never lose sight of the fact that most of the events of life are produced by combinations of transits, affecting radical and progressed places; and that no one transit over a single place is every productive of important events. it is always the combinations that are of consequence.

The very marked periods of a person's life are produced by the coincidence of two or three important transits over two or three important radical or progressed places; the planets transiting being those that hold significant places in the natus; especially when angular or when the places transited are angular. The most marked effects are (in regard to a single department of life when both the progressed and radical places of a planet, helio and geo., are either all afflicted at the same time or all benefitted at the same time. Also when both the radical and progressed Ascendant are attacked at the same time, etc., when, for instance, all four positions of Mercury are so attacked with very little assistance from favorable angles, and Mercury is radically afflicted, the tendency to nervous disorder is four places of Venus are so attacked by the malefics at the same a period of great unhappiness or grief is likely. Finally, when Sun, Moon, and Venus are all afflicted at the same time by transit, the consequences are likely to be very marked, indeed.

When the radical Sun is afflicted by Saturn, the progressed Sun being at the same time benefitted by the transit of Jupiter—even though Saturn does afflict the radical Sun by this transit (evil aspect) then the consequences, at least as long as Jupiter assists the progressed Sun, are not likely to be all serious, unless the radical Sun is very heavily afflicted at birth and the progressed Sun is in a position that also meets several evil aspects. Jupiter, normally, is well able to ward off the worst effects of Saturn so long as he continues near the aspect, but it must be remembered at the same time that no planet nullifies the action of any other planet.

Suppose the radical Sun is squared in transit by Saturn and trined by Jupiter; each of these bodies will have its particular effect, and while the square of Saturn will bring some misfortune into life; the trine of Jupiter will bring some good fortune which in the aggregate will greatly compensate for the evil done by Saturn. But will not really do away with the influence of that planet—Saturn will have his effect.

Transits of the Planet Jupiter

Jupiter in Favorable Aspect to Sun
These are among the most marked periods of the life, when the health is good, the spirits above par, everything is prosperous, and new opportunities are arising. Jupiter brings, when aspecting the Sun, times of recuperation, the attaining of one's object, financial improvement, and in all ways heads the ill effects of the malefics. Jupiter is in favorable aspect to the sun during a very large proportion of a person's life, and especially when you consider that the progressed Sun has also to be taken into account.

First, it is favorable for one's dealings with the male sex. The father, the husband, or any man intimate in the life. At this time the men associated with you closely are inclined to be happier more fortunate, in better health and spirits, and kinder, more considerate, and beneficial to you. It is a general signification of health and prosperity to the male side of the family.

It is favorable to any man with whom you are associated in business or in any way that is not strictly social. It is the best time in which to enter upon new relations with men, make partnerships, or to establish business connections. It usually brings into the life men who play a helpful and beneficial part in your destiny, and it also bring brings offers and opportunities in a business way to men, and sometimes offers of marriage to women. It is a splendid aspect under which to marry.

It is also favorable financially, one's money matters go along smoothly, and money comes in without delay, obstruction or trouble. It indicates freedom from delays and hindrances, and the clearing of the way for the accomplishment of ends. It always ushers in a better financial period, although if the radical Jupiter is afflicted at the same time by Saturn, the results from the financial standpoint may not be so marked.

It is also favorable for honors, attainment of position, and power, bestowal of favors, advance in rank, and in a general sense will materially aid in bringing your plans to completion. Whatever you undertake under this aspect is likely to succeed. If you inaugurate new movements under it, they are likely to prosper. Friendships made at this time are likely to prove beneficial.

Partnerships entered upon are satisfactory. For a woman, the men she meets and becomes interested in are likely to prove fortunate for her. Opportunities arising at this time should never be neglected and one should plan to take advantage of the periods of Jupiter to the fullest extent by putting oneself in line for meeting new people, by embracing opportunities, and by being open to suggestion, and chances that arise during this aspect. It is a time when one can safely take a chance, and it is very strong promise of sure success to enter upon an undertaking when Jupiter is making the approach to a sextile, trine, or conjunction of the Sun.

For a woman, it works out the same way. Provided that she is in any sense professionally employed, or in the business world, and as this is not usually the case, the aspect works out through her health and through her relations with the men with whom she is associated. It benefits the husband and all men who concern her intimately, even her sons though you will regard testimonies gathered from the fifth for sons, the third for brothers, and seventh for the husband, etc) and it indicates a period of success for them. it is the aspect par excellence of material prosperity, advantage, opportunity, and success.

Jupiter in Opposition or Square to Sun
This aspect, not usually noticed much by the astrologer, but certainly very important, is, in a general sense, favorable for health and spirits, making one cheerful, confident, and optimistic; but it tends to surfeit, congestion, and dispose tissue, and is not really and finally a favorable aspect at all. In the case of the square, it has a very misleading trait, which has led the astrologer to attribute to the square of the radical Jupiter to the Sun the benefits that belong to the trine and the sextile. This arises from the curious fact that when Jupiter is squaring the Sun geocentrically, he is quintile to the Sun heliocentrically, and when he is quintile to the Sun geocentrically, he is squaring the Sun heliocentrically, so there is a double aspect, and it will be better to reckon the square as not so evil as the opposition, as the latter will have no compensating aspect. In the case of the square, there are likely to be present some of the effects of the good aspects and some of the effects of the bad, although, of course, the consequences of the quintile can hardly be as powerful as those of the conjunction, trine, and sextile.

The tendency is toward the arising of opportunities that appear very favorable and in which one takes great stock and has high hopes, but the outcome is never satisfactory, there is often more expense than profit and hampering conditions. One is often obliged to put up with certain forms of limitation, particularly along lines of the species of circumstances where the conditions are outwardly favorable, apparently prosperous, and in which all the attendant incidents are well-appearing, but in connections with which one is dissatisfied, tied down, and restless. one has to submit to authority of those who follow what one knows to be false standards, wrong, or mistaken methods, to be annoyed by various harassing conditions, and always in such a way that the thing on the outside seems to be all right and has much to commend it. one of the chief concomitants is increased expense, misled ambitions, and aspirations, ambitions directed in the wrong channels, and one finally finds out that one cannot get along that way.

This is a poor time for important financial matters, for entering upon new enterprises, for attempting to gratify one's ambitions, for expecting increase, advance, and honors. It is also a poor time for legal affairs, and for dealing with people of wealth and power, and while it may bring certain opportunities into the life, they are never very satisfactory.

Jupiter in Conjunction or Favorable Aspect to Moon
This is singularly fortunate for one's dealings with the public, for travel, and for domestic affairs, for personal happiness, for one's relations with women, and usually at this time some woman plays a very important and helpful part in the life. It is very favorable for the health and affairs of the wife, mother, or any woman intimate in the life, and is a harmonizing, peaceful influence under which your private and personal affairs are likely to be well ordered, your senses under control, your instincts normal, and it favors conservatism, regard for the conventions, improved ways of living, well regulated habits, and good health.

It is a very fortunate time in which to make domestic changes, and any made at this time are likely to be fortunate. It is a fortunate time in which to make the acquaintance of women, and favors, and kindnesses are likely to come through them. Any woman entering your life at this time is sure to beneficial, a good influence, and likely to assist you in some financial way. If your domestic affairs are at all involved, and, in the case of a man, his matrimonial affairs, this aspect serves to straighten things out, and in every way it operates favorably upon the private life. At this time your emotional nature is more under control, your feelings are directed into more healthy and normal channels, and it's a time for reform, of reconstruction, and the abandonment of evil courses. It is of course, especially favorable for the health of a woman. People whose business connects them with the general public will benefit at this time, especially politicians, and the like. It is a fortunate aspect under which to marry, for a man.

Jupiter in Evil Aspect to Moon
Your domestic affairs at this time will be well-ordered, but you are likely to be hampered and interfered with at this time by influences which are too conservative, too conventional, and people who are too much taken up with the externals of life. You are likely to be compelled, for the time, to follow certain lines of action of which you do not approve and to hold yourself in check, and act in a more conventional manner than is you wont. It is unfavorable for the health and affairs of the wife or mother and domestic affairs are likely to be expensive, and there may be a tendency at this time for too much display, extravagance, and show. This is not a very important aspect, but quite annoying in some ways.

Jupiter in Conjunction or Favorable Aspect to Mercury
Under this aspect, you will receive stimulus toward mental advancement, and particularly in the direction of making of practical use the knowledge you have or of acquiring the more practical end of any subject, in which you may be interested. For instance, suppose that you are interested in astrology, and you have the transit of Uranus over your Mercury, this will cause you to seek for new ideas, to extend the theoretical knowledge, and to know, and understand more about the more difficult problems, to try experiments, enter upon research work, etc., but the aspect of Jupiter will cause you to feel that you want, now, to bring all your knowledge to a practical standpoint, to make it useful and profitable, and since Jupiter is the planet of finance, and of practical constructiveness, you can readily see that it causes you to treat your knowledge in such a way as to make it useful, and so it does not mean the acquisition of new ideas so much as the ordering, application extension, and practical understanding of the old ones.

You will increase your stock of useful knowledge, you will increase your efficiency and practical ability, and but the time the aspect has passed on, you will be in a better position to use the time and profit by the ideas you had. It causes one to study, to reach out for learning, to consult authorities, to reduce their ideas to system, to listen to the advice and counsel of others, to be more tolerant and more amenable to reason and less critical, less incredulous, and it usually brings someone into the life whose knowledge, advice, and encouragement aid one in this task. It is a splendid aspect under which to take definite courses of study, especially those prescribed by authority, and to reach out for mental honors. It favors writing, correspondence, and all legal affairs, it is fine for the judgement, it is a good time in which to make important decisions which will influence your future, and in every way it brightens up, vitalizes and makes efficient the action of the mind. It is a most important influence, a good aspect under which to speak or write, to publish, advertise, but the most important influence is what has already been mentioned, namely, to enable you to put your ideas into shape.

For example, while Uranus was in aspect to Mercury, I would think up new ideas, investigate theories, invent and make them practical, put them in right shape for use, complete them, fill out all the details, and market them. So, under this aspect, people are likely to improve their working methods, business men are likely to improve, and put to rights office management, and it is also favorable aspect for one's relations with employees, especially clerks, and the like. It frees one from worry, makes minor matters go smoothly, and means content, satisfaction, and cheerfulness. It removes nervousness, irritability, and fretfulness, gives confidence, social ability, and causes one's relations with people generally to be more satisfactory.

Jupiter Afflicting Mercury
This is a bad time for legal affairs and litigation, bad for making important decisions affecting matters of finance, and tends to loss,

worry over money and property, and while not a disastrous aspect, or very evil, tends to a condition of affairs which is very unsatisfactory, because the mind is in a very sanguine condition, one's hopes and expectations will hardly be realized. It tends to wrong conceptions, causes one to be compelled to exercise the mind on matters which are hardly interesting, or really profitable, associates one with people who try one's patience, and annoys one with their red tape, officious, conventionality, etc., and it is quite an annoying aspect. Unless Mercury is afflicted at birth or by direction, it is not necessary to expect much of this aspect. It is, however, unwise to enter legal matters, or undertake important correspondence or study under this aspect.

Jupiter in Conjunction or Good Aspect to Venus
This is one of the most favorable transits that can occur in a minor way in the nativity. It brings new friends, pleasant social affairs, presents, favors, happiness, personal comfort and contentment, invitation, kindness and consideration from friends, and usually brings someone into the life who plays a helpful part, particularly in the way of stirring up and gratifying the better and more wholesome side of the emotional nature. It is a very healthy satisfactory influence, and tends towards relations that are at the same time perfectly in accord with the conventions and perfectly pleasant in every respect. It favors visits to old friends, intercourse with relatives, and one's home, and it is a very good aspect under which to visit old friends or relatives, to effect reconciliations, marriages, and all social affairs, artistic affairs, and it indicates in the lives of the artistic, gain, and success through their particular art. It always brings pleasurable and beneficial experiences into the life and is socially constructive.

This is the time to extend your acquaintance, to select friends, to broaden your social horizon, and to take up the broken threads of interrupted friendships, particularly will it be quite sure to bring some very pleasant influence into the life, whether male or female, someone who will minister top your pleasure, afford you considerable happiness, and in a general way make life happier for you. You will be in a mood for enjoyment, and yet inclined to seek normal and healthy forms of it, and it's influence is strongly against any form of pleasure which is not wholesome. This will especially apply to the trine, sextile, and quintile, as the conjunction, if it occurs in a place where there are many afflicting aspects meeting, it may not be able to overcome the abnormal tendencies, but it will at least throw its influence in that direction.

It is under this aspect that people take fresh courage, get young and more spontaneous, attend to their dress and appearance, are more magnetic, more cheerful and more social, and naturally seek the fellowship of their kind. It nearly always brings favors, kindness and presents. It is always wise to plan for some trip, important social affairs, important artistic matters, holidays, and journeys for pleasure. Visits to people of whom you are fond, marriages, when you see this aspect coming on, as no matters of this sort can go very badly under this aspect unless there are contradictory aspects of a very powerful sort.

Jupiter in Evil Aspect to Venus
If you refer to the contrary aspect, namely Venus to evil aspect of Jupiter, you will get the coloring of this, without the necessity of repeating all the details. It ushers in a period where you are apt to be associated with people who bore you with their over-conventional attitude. You are likely to have a great many invitations, favors, and even presents that you do not want and would rather be without, and it has a sort of stifling effect that a close room overheated has. Of course, it is not in every horoscope that these effects come out quite so strongly, but that is the phase of the aspect.

Jupiter in Conjunction or Evil Aspect to Mars
It seems to me that I gave you this; but in case not, here it is. This is expansive to the feelings and emotions, leads to acts of courage, unselfishness, religious enthusiasm, generosity, and disregard for money, and tends to extravagance, carelessness, and sometimes

loss. It is, in a general way, threatening financially, as all of Jupiter's aspects are to planets by square, opposition, or semi-square, or an afflicted conjunction. I was robbed under the following configuration: Jupiter entering Scorpio opposite Neptune and Mars radical and square to Mercury, helio, with Saturn entering Taurus in opposition. It was through sheer carelessness, as I did not properly guard my things, and thought it perfectly safe to leave things exposed. The conjunction or favorable aspects to Mars are good for soldiers, doctors, surgeons, and those who follow Mars professions, or are engaged in work of a dangerous, enterprising or arduous nature, where the principles of courage, strength, and initiative are called out.

Jupiter in Conjunction or Good Aspect to Saturn
This is not important and tends to economy, prudence, and care in matters of finance. This aspect is restrictive, and produces nothing positive, but favors dealings with old people, things connected with old conditions, the earth, real estate, mines, house, or land property, and is a very good time to start a bank account, enter upon financial matters with regard to one's distant future, etc.

Jupiter in Evil Aspect to Saturn
This is a slightly restricting, unfavorable aspect for financial matters in general, and is a delaying, hampering, and interesting aspect. It slows down the benefic rays of Jupiter, and if Jupiter is making the good aspect to some part of the horoscope, and it meets this aspect, it must to a large extent prevent the full effect of Jupiter and slow down his vibrations. It is an annoying aspect, but not of the greatest importance as good aspects to the radical place of Jupiter can easily offset the influence.

Jupiter in Good Aspect or Conjunction to Uranus
This favors financial gain through inventions, discoveries, new enterprises, corporations, etc., and sometimes brings money unexpectedly, and through peculiar means. If the place of Uranus is much afflicted, beware of the conjunction as it may bring sudden

and unlooked for losses, and cause financial fluctuations of a very spasmodic order. Brought to Uranus or Saturn, the good aspects of Jupiter sometimes bring inheritances or legacies.

Jupiter in Evil Aspect to Uranus
This is a very uncertain influence, and at this time money you expect may not come to you, or you may have strange losses or unexpected misfortune, in a financial way. The aspects of Jupiter to the superiors have these effects financially, but not in the degree that the aspects of the superiors to the body of Jupiter do. At the same time, when Jupiter squares, or opposes Uranus it is a poor time in which to take chances, speculate, or play in games of chance where money is involved. The same is true when Jupiter afflicts Mars.

Jupiter in Conjunction or Evil Aspect to Neptune
This awakes the altruistic side of the nature, makes one charitable and more unselfish, and one is likely under this influence to give to charity, to spend money on the needy, and to generally be easy and readily bamboozled. It is a very spiritualizing influence, and often awakens the religious side of the nature to a great extent. It leads in the direction of a purer and more spiritual form of belief, and worship, and inclines one to all they can make practical the spirit of Christianity. This in superior horoscopes, of course. It's chief danger, otherwise, is in its subjecting one to feelings of generosity and compassion that are apt to be misused and taken advantage of by others.

Transits of the Planet Saturn

As the chief instrument in the Universe of all the ills that flesh is heir to, Saturn easily takes the prize for making trouble, and his aspects, as he slowly wends his way around the horoscope, are always productive of some form of discipline, sorrow, and affliction.

Saturn in Conjunction or Evil Aspect to Sun
First of all, this has a debilitating effect upon the constitution, lowers the vitality, and makes one susceptible to any diseases to which one is subject. It is a depressing and devitalizing influence, and one of the chief causes of ill health. The transit of Saturn in the first house of the horoscope is similar in this respect, lowering the whole vibratory rate of the individual. Nothing goes just right under this condition (to the Sun) and everything slows down, is delayed, and meets with obstacles and hindrances. It not only affects your health, but is also evil for the health and conditions of the males closely connected in your domestic or business life. Sometimes it brings about marked changes and even deaths. Everything is retarded at this time, and in order to accomplish anything, you have to make more effort than usual and you are easily discouraged, easily tired, and often misunderstood and blamed for things

for which you are really not responsible. It brings blame from superiors, and troubles in employment. It is wise at this time to take things as they come and try not to force conditions. You cannot at this time be too careful whom you trust in business, and this is the very worst time in the world to initiate new ventures, start any important undertaking, or enter into any new relations with men. To a woman, it brings general inharmony in the married life, trouble and misunderstandings with the husband, fiancé, or lover, and is a very bad condition under which to enter into relations with men, become engaged, married, or enter into any agreement whatsoever. New men that come into the life are likely to turn out disappointing to the end. If nothing more, it brings some broken friendship through misunderstanding.

The best advice in regard to this aspect is the following: first, guard the health, and see that you do not get run down, anaemic, or below par. Second, do not force conditions, and when delays and obstacles spring up, do not try to forcibly sweep them away. Next, do not enter into partnership with a man or become engaged, married, or enter into partnership with a man, or become engaged, married, or enter into intimate relations under this aspect, as he will bring you sorrow, responsibility, care and worry, and perhaps deceive you in the bargain. He is likely to be married, or in some way tied up so that he can not in any case really belong to you. Next, avoid misunderstandings with the men in your life at this time, and do not allow Saturn to make you too dissatisfied with existing conditions.

This aspect does not necessarily affect the financial conditions, although it may do so and will if Jupiter is also afflicted at the same time. But the usual way it works is to make you dissatisfied with existing conditions, have trouble with men with whom you are associated, want to change your employment, and if married, sick, and tired of your husband who will not be very magnetic, agreeable, or pleasing under this aspect. It would thus be very easy to make a great mistake. As soon as the aspect passes, things will readjust themselves. If men treat you wrongly or unjustly, this will straighten out when the aspect is past. Until then, take the line of least resistance, be patient, and wait for the dawn.

Saturn in Good Aspect to Sun
This is very unimportant, slightly restrictive, and tends to moderation, prudence, and caution. It may serve to hold back otherwise unfavorable conditions, and is wholly negative.

Saturn in Evil Aspect or Conjunction to Moon
This is also evil for the health, but in a functional way, and is likely to bring on troubles such as are signified by the Moon's sign at birth, or other planets which afflict this point. It is depressing and discouraging in a personal way, unfavorable for domestic affairs, and productive of trouble with or through women. You may be anxious over the health or affairs of some woman in your life at this time, such as the mother or wife, or else you may have trouble with or on account of some woman. Some woman may be jealous of you, take occasion to dislike you, treat you wrongfully, or abuse you, and at this time, no matters in which women are concerned in your life can turn out satisfactorily.

You will be dissatisfied with your environment, either want to travel, or else do so, and it is always a heavy, dull, unhappy, or uninspired period from the private and personal standpoint. There will be something in the home or private life that is a source of anxiety or unhappiness. Some woman may pass out of your life, and sometimes it brings the death of the mother or wife. It is always a bad time for a married man, and at this time his wife will be sick, disagreeable, or a cause of worry and trouble. In the case of women, they will also have trouble with or through their own sex.

A man should not marry under this aspect or enter into relations with women as in this case they will in the end prove a burden, bring unhappiness into their life, and play a restricting part. It is also evil for dealings with the public, as for instance in the case of a politician, who depends on the public vote. It brings unpopularity, and sometimes, in the case of the afflicted Moon, disgrace. The women who enter your life at this time are bound to disappoint you and cause you worry, unhappiness, and trouble.

Saturn in Favorable Aspect to Moon
This is good for dealings with elderly women, and tends to self-control, caution and prudence in private affairs and control of the senses. It is not important.

Saturn in Conjunction or Evil Aspect to Mercury
This is very disturbing to the mentality and depressing, too, and the memory and concentration are poor, while the tendency is to try very hard to overcome obstacles because Saturn is a plodder. It tends to pessimism, incredulity, and skepticism, unbelief, doubt mental distress, and the careful examination of your mental outfit, with a view to throwing out whatever seems unfit. It causes people to change their point of view on many matters, to question matters they have held for a long time, and during this aspect you are likely to very uneasy, unhappy, and rather subject to moods and the "blues." It tends to mental effort, hard study, and patient effort that, however, results in little benefit unless there is some good aspect at the same time. At this time, avoid the law, litigation, and disputes, and be careful of what you put in writing. Your correspondence is likely to be unsatisfactory, and it is well not to ask for favors in writing as you would be likely to put things in such a way that no good will follow. This aspect sometimes brings important changes and journeys. It also tends toward trouble with the voice and colds in the throat and chest.

Saturn here sometimes brings someone into the life whose views and opinions have a very detrimental and worrying effect upon you, and owing to whom you become unsettled. You are bound, under this aspect, to have cause for worry, depression, and fear, and some circumstance is sure to come up to cause it. It may bring very serious and harassing conditions where Mercury is much afflicted at birth. It is a poor time under which to undertake studies, writing, or speaking.

Saturn in Good Aspect to Mercury
This tends to mental continuity, patience, perseverance, and careful, earnest study, and though quite negative, is good but not very important.

Saturn in Conjunction or Evil Aspect to Venus
This is one of the most disagreeable aspects in the whole range, but as you know, if the place of Venus is not afflicted, it will not work out in full force. It causes a person to be more sensitive, easily slighted, and more exacting with those around him or her than is usually the case, and you will be led to feel that people do not care for you as much as they should, etc. One expects too much of their friends, and when they are not able to meet your demands, you may feel hurt, become indifferent, and disposed to magnify and brood over slights and neglects that may not be intended or are caused by circumstances that are beyond their control. Any feeling of jealousy should be avoided, and if you feel that your friends are treating you with less consideration than usual, be sure, first of all, that you are not imagining two-thirds of it, and in the next place that your own attitude is not responsible for the remainder. Remember that the harboring of such thoughts is sure to drive away from you the very ones you wish most to hold.

This aspect seldom passes without some sorrow, whether in the form of death of someone dear to you or the separation from someone you love. New friends made at this time are likely to bring more sorrow or discipline into the life than pleasure or benefit. This aspect of Saturn to Venus is very unfavorable for social affairs, which do not go rightly, and you will be disappointed in things not turning out pleasantly. The people you wish to meet will not be presented to you or your plans for pleasure will be disappointed. It is an unhappy influence under which to play and for gaiety, amusement, or anything of the sort, and it is unwise to expect much from a vacation, a social engagement, a visit, a meeting between friends, or a love affair, marriage, or anything that concerns the personal happiness under this condition. Do not marry, become engaged, or arrange for any important social meeting under this aspect. It is particularly bad for artists, actors, and musicians as well as poets or all those whose work depends upon art. At this time their work will not be satisfactory; they will not be magnetic, and their efforts are not likely to be crowned with success.

It would be the height of folly to plan for a concert, entertainment, reading a dramatic work, or anything of that nature under this aspect unless there are very strong contradictory aspects, as for instance, if Saturn were square Venus, Jupiter trine another planet, and Uranus assisting another. In all cases it is very evil for Saturn to be afflicting the radical places as this leaves more permanent results for evil. In cases where Jupiter were benefitting one, but Saturn afflicting the other, you might expect some good results but some setbacks, and owing to Jupiter, the thing might be financially satisfactory, but owing to Saturn it would go off rather dully and not be altogether a credit. In a personal way, friends met under this influence are sure to be disappointing in some way and it is an evil omen unless powerfully contradicted.

Saturn in Favorable Aspect to Venus
This is unimportant, tends to control the affection, regulate the emotions, form associations with older and more serious people, and is a purely negative influence. It does work in the direction of preventing unwise impulsive attachments, and adds to the power to withstand temptation and set with caution and prudence in matters of the affections.

Saturn in Conjunction or Unfavorable Aspect to Mars
This is apt to make one feel abused and ill treated, and sometimes brings treachery and stirs up jealousy and enmity. One should avoid feeling bitter, revengeful, and also avoid cruelty, unfeeling acts, and unkindness, as well as an unforgiving spirit. It is apt to

bring very trying experiences, to make one's work difficult or arduous and often is very important, and must not be overlooked. People under this aspect are apt to feel abusive, very bitter toward the world, and express themselves rather harshly and vindictively.

Saturn in Favorable Aspect to Mars
This aspect is not important except as a restraining force and tends to regulate the impulses.

Saturn in Conjunction or Evil Aspect to Jupiter
This aspect tends toward economy, prudence, caution, and circumspection of financial matters in conjunction. It slows all financial affairs and often brings a period in which matters of this sort are delayed and hindered, and money is scarce or expenses large. Usually when anyone is in financial straits, Saturn is afflicting Jupiter. It does not tend so much to loss as it does to expense, small returns, delayed payments, etc. This is an unfavorable time for investments or for taking chances where money is concerned, and you will be sure to do the wrong thing.

Everything at this time tends to lower the bank account. If you own property, it will need repairs, be an anxiety, or decrease in value. It is a poor time for building or buying real estate. It is also a poor time also for reaching for honors and getting involved with the law, and it is best at this time to be diplomatic, settle disputes out of court, and run no financial risks. It lessens one's faith in oneself and the Universe, and destroys confidence. During the period of Saturn's affliction to Jupiter, especially if the place of Jupiter is afflicted, a good deal of financial trouble is likely to result, and it is a good thing to have the two places of Jupiter well separated so that Saturn cannot get at them at the same time. This aspect is unfavorable for the liver as it makes it sluggish, and you should avoid biliousness. In conjunction where Jupiter is not afflicted, it is good for economy, real estate, matters of land and house property, and all affairs where returns are slow and sure.

Saturn in Favorable Aspect to Jupiter

This aspect favors care, thrift, saving, and caution in financial matters, and is also good for real estate, farms, house and land, mines, etc. This is a good aspect under which to invest in some slow, sure form of investment, and anything of the nature of Saturn.

Transits of the Planet Uranus

If the transits of Jupiter are the most beneficial and those of Saturn the most unfortunate, those of Uranus are the most important and interesting. Uranus is the developer and the bringer to the surface of latent possibilities, and he augments the powers of the planets he aspects to the ninth power.

If any point in the horoscope awaits development, there is nothing that will bring it out more than the transits of Uranus, and there is nothing that will afford experiences of the unusual type more readily than the conjunction and adverse aspects of this planet. The greatest opportunities of life come, as a rule, from the conjunction, trine, and sextile of the Sun, and the periods in which this aspect rules are always marked. If the Sun is aspected favorably, it becomes very important.

This is a very important transit and, first of all, will bring people into the life who will afford the means of developing and utilizing the latent possibilities. It stirs up the ambitions and activities, awakens the latent energies, and supplies the means of enlarging the sphere of influence, and bringing the native in contact with larger affairs than ever before experienced. It often connects one with governmental matters or corporations, and with inventions, untried enterprises, and undertakings of a unique and unusual sort. Anything may come of this aspect, and as this in the nature of Uranus to bring the unexpected into the life, whatever happens is likely to be not in accord with preconceived plans, and one may expect unexpected. Opportunities drop from the clouds.

This is a very constructive influence, and a very propitious time for having dealings with people of unusual ability, unique characters, and those whose interests are Universal, and who are concerned in large undertakings. It favors preferment, and the realization of hopes, wishes, and ambitions you may have been cherishing for years, and this aspect seldom passes without bringing opportunities of an unusual sort that should not be neglected as they are likely to lead to large developments. You will meet new people. Under this transit, people of large caliber always enter the life, and it is for you to utilize them, and let them utilize you. It increases the powers, ambitions, nervous energies, and efficiency, and it is likely to be a most active and interesting time generally.

To a woman, this aspect also presents great opportunities. It usually brings into the life men of power and prominence. It is highly fortunate for any man who might be in her life at the time, whether the father, husband, or otherwise, and indicates success, increased power and opportunity, and the possibility of their advancement and promotion. Under this influence, a woman is more magnetic, has more power over the men in her life, and is in every way more powerful for the time. It is impossible to say just what it will bring or just what peculiar changes may take place in order to bring about the desired advancement, but it is always favorable and a very active influence. It is a good time for her to seek favors from men of wealth, power, and ability, and to further both her own interests and those of any man in her life. Any man coming into the life under this influence is likely to play a very important, helpful, and interesting part, and to appeal to the highest and best in her.

Uranus in Square, Opposition or Afflicted Conjunction to Sun
This is a very disturbing influence that first of all leads to nervous diseases and complaints of the obscure kind that the average physician finds it hard to diagnose or cure. Next, it arouses and intensifies the ambitions, makes a person restless, dissatisfied with old conditions and conventional ways of doing things, and turns the ambitions in the direction of untried, novel, and sometimes impracticable undertakings, mostly connected with inventions, discoveries, out-of-the-way ideas, matters connected with corporations and the government, and usually the ideas one has regarding these things are unsafe, much too sanguine, too ahead of the times, and impracticable.

One is likely to be thrown with people who encourage these ideas and who are either misled, fraudulent, or else totally unwise. It is often a cause for a man to be very ill-advised and always he advocates the unpopular cause, the thing that can never be attained, and he feels inclined to force issues, to put his individual will against the world-will, which Uranus in a sense represents, and the result is bound to be disastrous. One is led to take unusual and extraordinary points of view, and to antagonize those with whom one works, associates, or business dealings, and the usual result is the loss of friends, especially the safe and sane ones, and those who are really trustworthy. One is left the victim of the woozy, the dishonest, and the dissatisfied.

It is impossible for a man under this aspect to feel satisfied with things, and it is also impossible for things to be satisfactory. The aspect is, in its nature, confusing and worrying, leading to intense activity, usually misdirected, and therefore productive of anxiety, great expenditure of energies, and nothing to show for it. Things seem to promise well to the last minute and then fall through without a moment's warning. Nothing can really be trusted that is not strictly along the lines of the greatest conservatism and nothing of a new, venturesome order ought to be taken up at this time. But that, of course, is just what will be taken up.

It causes sudden deaths, separations, and misunderstandings with the family life or the business life, on the male side always. The father or business partner may die, or something unexpected and unlooked for usually eventuates at this time, always from the most unexpected quarter. In very well balanced horoscopes, the aspect might pass without much disturbance, but where the Sun is at all afflicted, such will be the case, and it is quite the most radical and extreme of all the transits. The thing to do is not to allow oneself to make important changes under this influence as it is totally misleading, and any important change made under it is not likely to turn out well at all, but be disastrous.

In the case of a woman, it is very disturbing to the married life, usually brings about misunderstandings and sometimes death of the husband. But it always complicates things, being evil for the business interests of the husband, and health and affairs of the man in the life, and usually brings some very strong influence into the life in the way of a man who is a fascination in some way, a great temptation, and a danger the future interests. Under this aspect, women are led astray, leave their husbands, and do all sorts of foolish things, and if married, the husband at this time is likely to be a severe trial, and things go very wrong. Usually a man enters the life, is married, or at least has not honorable intentions. To the unmarried, it frequently brings a marriage or an engagement that ends disastrously, and the influence that comes in under this aspect does not last long. As a rule, it enters very suddenly and leaves as suddenly and usually in some peculiar way, and the first meeting usually is more or less unconventional. It is the worst possible influence under which to become engaged, marry, or enter into relations with a man, and nothing permanently good can possibly come of it.

The main things for both men and women are the following: Do not take up new schemes, or if you do, do not expect things to turn out as you plan them. Do not plan too far ahead, for Fate will overturn all your plans. Expect the unexpected. Do not trust new people. People who approach you in a business way, or with enterprises, are unreliable so watch out for yourself. Do not overdo or you will have a nervous breakdown. Avoid the impossible, the impractical, the new and visionary, and be as sane, safe, conservative, and humdrum as possible. Be prepared to accept the inevitable. (This is the aspect that destroyed Teddy Roosevelt.)

Uranus in Conjunction or Evil Aspect to Moon
The conjunction with an afflicted Moon is as disturbing to man as the Sun is to a woman. It upsets the domestic life, usually causes ill health of the wife or mother or some woman in the life, and turns the private life upside down. A man is lucky if there is not some form of scandal connected with it all. The wife is apt to have some nervous complaint, be ill, or in some way upset the serenity of the home. She may die suddenly. The death is likely of a woman intimate in the life or home circle. Whatever happens will be unexpected and come about suddenly, and all domestic plans are likely to be upset at this time. The influence of Uranus here is very disturbing to the personal life, and some woman is likely to come into the life and play a very disturbing part, perhaps causing a lot of trouble, but also be very fascinating. Men under this aspect sometimes have love affairs or sometimes their wives do unusual things. It always brings some woman into the life who has a strong influence and comes suddenly, and in all cases there is a disordered state. The wife, mother, or another woman is always a course of worry. It is unfavorable for dealings with the public, and sometimes brings on nervous complaints, as will be indicated by the Moon's sign and the planets afflicting her.

Women have peculiar experiences through their own gender. They usually have some strong female influence in their life that is not for the best and that is misleading and productive of disturbance and trouble and sometimes ends in sudden misunderstanding, jealousy, and separation. It is a great disturbance in the personal and private life.

Uranus Trine, Sextile, or Conjunction Moon
When to a well-aspected Moon, this tends to travel and interesting experiences, and brings women into the life through whom one gains mentally, gets a wider, and more comprehensive viewpoint. It has the general tendency to broaden the mental and spiritual horizon. This takes place through the help of women as a rule. One woman plays a very important and helpful part in the life at this time, and "initiates" the native into bigger and better things. In 1901, with Uranus trine Moon, a woman who was not interested in astrology took it upon herself to send me all books she could get of an astrological nature and "mothered" my mental development as best she could. I was so situated that I could not do this for myself at the time. She gave me absolute *carte blanche*, and through her I was able to study and get well under way. This is the sort of thing this aspect does, and always the influence is very disinterested, humanitarian, unselfish, and acting along high and broad lines.

It sometimes acts in a very occult manner, and always is for the uplifting, ennobling, and expanding of the mind and soul. It is splendid for the wife and mother, and for all women in your life at the time. Women with this transit are apt to become interested in clubs, large movements, and humanitarian interests, and sometimes travel, and always expand and enlarge their horizons. It works, as Uranus always does, unexpectedly, in peculiar ways, and does strange things. It is rather a subjective aspect unless other planets are in the aspect, such as Mars, Jupiter, or Venus, and one hardly realizes what is happening at the time. During the period I absorbed the bigger ideas of life, consumed astrology, and laid the real foundation for all my future work.

**Uranus in Conjunction to Afflicted Mercury,
or Square or Opposition Mercury**
This is a very disturbing influence indeed, leading to nervous complications which arise largely from worried and confused mental conditions and too great excitability. The mental affairs are likely at this time to be most active, very disordered, and distracting.

Correspondence goes awry, with things happening unexpectedly and the tendency is in every way to throw the mind into the greatest activity and confusion. At this time one is apt to feel very much out of harmony with one's usual associates and accustomed ideas, and the mind is reaching out for new lines of thought, new experience and knowledge. You feel restless, nervous, unsettled, and cranky. The judgment is not likely to be as conservative or safe as usual and the memory is treacherous; this is thus a poor time to make important decisions.

The subconscious mind is more active, and one may have unaccountable moods and sensations and some unusual experience along mental lines, and it will be very hard for you to stick to routine. It is likely that one will take up with new and peculiar ideas and be led astray by ideas that are impractical and visionary. Avoid being sarcastic, disagreeable, and too critical. You may, by adopting too radical an attitude and being too extreme in the expression of your opinions, antagonize your associates and have quarrels and misunderstandings with the people you ordinarily talk and live with, and this may lead to your making unwise changes in regard to your friends and associations. It tends to travel, and some sort of change is sure to arrive. It means mental expansion, and whatever is necessary to bring this about will take place.

This aspect tends to notoriety in the press, advertising, or some form of publicity, and may bring unpleasant criticism or involve one in some controversy, legal complications, or some form of worry that will be very harassing and annoying. Avoid quarrels, disputes, and the law and try and be cautious in what you say and do, as you are most likely to express yourself unconventionally, be misunderstood, misquoted, libeled, and generally talked about for your crazy notions. Be guarded as to what studies you take up, or what ideas you follow, as you are more than likely to be led astray.

In the case of the conjunction, a great deal of judgment is required, as is really the case with all conjunctions, and the meaning of the conjunction is, of course, great mental development, and it will largely depend upon the aspects as to whether it will be beneficial or not. In any case, new forms of thought and study, and new mental experiences of the most interesting sort will take place. You will try mental experiments, take up untried ideas, and meet with people who will give you the impetus for branching out. Important transits to Mercury are usually indicative of people coming into the life who associate with you, whether in connection with business or social life.

On the mental plane, it gives one the means of development, stimulates thought, and introduces new ideas. With the conjunction of Uranus to Mercury at the present time, I have been constantly thrown with people who are presenting ideas of various sorts to me, and who are talking about matters of an occult nature, and my mind is in just the state to take up some new line of thought. I am also doing a certain amount of speaking and getting a little publicity. You, with Mercury conjunct Uranus radically, always have a certain amount of this sort of thing. The tendency is to make the mental life more interesting, to develop the intellect, to afford new experience, to improve the expression and bring the mind to its fullest development. The conjunction favors writing, lecturing, publicity of all sorts, and travel. Some dominant influence is likely to be felt at this time, and someone may come who is able to instruct and assist the intellectual life.

Uranus Trine and Sextile Mercury
This is very favorable for mental advancement, activity in the intellectual realm, new friends in research, and an added interest in science, ideas out of the common, and all things that tend to develop the mind. It quickens the abilities, causes one to learn and absorb readily and to be open to new ideas and the advice and counsel of others. You readily adopt new plans and methods for the management of your affairs and are more responsive to suggestions than at other times. You are likely to be brought into contact with people of an inventive, scientific, and progressive turn of

mind, and profit by association with them. Correspondence, writing and publicity are favored, as are legal affairs, the press, and scientific and literary matters, and this is a good time to advertise and gain publicity. Under this influence you say the right thing and expresses yourself in the best way. This is favorable for thinking up new ideas, inventions, dealings with the government and clients or customers, and the management of anything that requires quick and able mental action. It is good for lecturers, reporters, writers, journalists, and all those who use the pen largely in their pursuits.

This aspect usually brings some strong influence into the life in the way of a friend or associate who stimulates one's thoughts, awakens one's mind, and encourages one in broadening and developing. It is a good time in which to take up new studies and lines of thought, and in the case of people who are not intellectual, they usually adopt new and better methods of running their business, such as installing new systems, or bookkeeping, indexing, etc. so as to make their mental work easier. Or, they may listen to the suggestions of some scientific person and improve their way of living or working through some means of an advanced sort. Under this aspect, people are more than usually clever, ingenious, active, alert, and alive, and the mind works at its best.

Under the sextile of Uranus to Mercury, Uranus being in Sagittarius on the Ascendant, I met one of the greatest friends of my life who assisted me in developing my mind, encouraged me in many ways, and by talking about things with me, "fertilized" my intelligence. Uranus in Sagittarius was sextile my Mercury and conjunct his Mercury at the time of contact. We met on the deck of an ocean steamer and both recognized the other instantaneously as a much kindred mind, and from that moment, for eleven years we were in constant touch. He having the Moon square Saturn, finally, when Uranus left him high and dry, slumped mentally, and I went ahead of him so rapidly after a while that I knew I had to leave him behind. He wouldn't interest me for a moment now, and he would think I was "buggy." But under the temporary stimulus of Uranus, he was brilliant, fertile, original, and daring mentally, and for a time we made it warm for everyone. This was the time when I first woke up mentally and was one of the means employed.

The important transits to Mercury, especially if Jupiter and Uranus, usually bring, as I have said, important influences into the life that act upon the mind and cause development. The greatest friendship that can happen will come under a combination where Uranus transits to aspects of Mercury, showing mental contact, while Venus is also transited by Uranus or Jupiter, showing emotional contact. Or, perhaps Jupiter will be transiting Mercury by good aspect or conjunction and Uranus to good aspect of Venus. In other words, Jupiter and Uranus being the great opportunities, and the time when they are in concert with Venus and Mercury are always times when you have the most interesting people in your life, and when you are associated with people who understand you, and who enter into your real life.

Uranus in Adverse Aspect to Mercury
Avoid legal matters as you will the plague, and do all possible to keep the nervous system in good order. Avoid sudden changes which are "notional," and be guided by best judgment. Do not trust new ideas, and if you have an interest in brilliant people, admire the brilliance and take it for what it is worth.

Uranus Conjunction (well aspected), Trine, or Sextile Venus
This is one of the most important influences socially and personally and makes one very magnetic and disposed to be more conventional than usual in matters of social life, friendship, and affection, especially in the case of the conjunction, and attentive to matters of dress, personal attractiveness, and culture. The tendency is to develop the social side of life to its utmost, to broaden the acquaintance, and to break away from the narrow or limited environment, and there is a strong desire for companionship, love, and sympathy, and a strong personal interest. This usually comes in the form of someone who plays a very fascinating part in the life, and

it all depends upon the horoscope as to whether it will be a very conventional "affair" or a friendship or love affair of the very highest type.

In a great many cases, this brings in the greatest and most tremendous love of the whole life, and especially if at the same time there are powerful aspects to Venus by direction, especially of the Sun, or Mars, so that Uranus in aspecting Venus, also gets the aspect of other planets. It is also very fortunate to have, either radically or at this time the conjunction, trine, or sextile of Mercury to Venus so that both are included in the aspect, when great mental as well as emotional and esthetic development may be expected, and a great deal of pleasure, happiness, and intercourse of the most interesting and profitable sort. The person who comes into the life under this aspect understands you, and seems to get more in touch with you than is ordinarily the case, and the contact of Uranus with Venus keys up the emotions, the aesthetic sentiments, and the social feelings to the utmost so that you are more magnetic, more in the mood for pleasure, and more able to take advantage of a great friendship than would ordinarily be the case.

In less advanced horoscopes, this will bring unusual experiences, great happiness, and a very unconventional period of social life, and tend toward experiences and contact with people that are beyond the power of the person to either control, appreciate, or live up to, and as soon as the aspect dies out, they will be left behind. It is the greatest time for forming interesting attachments that may be made to last a lifetime, but the tendency of Uranus is to bring the unexpected, and the hero or heroine of the occasion is quite likely to arrive suddenly, unexpectedly, and somewhat unconventionally. It may be love at first sight, but in any case, there is instant recognition, the feeling you have known the person before, or some peculiar and marked psychic or intuitive incident in connection with the meeting. They swiftly come to a climax as a rule, the friendship progressing by leaps and bounds, and the mutual attraction is intense but not feverish in the case of the sextile or trine.

The conjunction is overpowering, and unless Venus is well protected by Jupiter, Saturn, or other favorable aspects, the person is likely to act unwisely, break all conventions and let his or her emotional nature play the deuce with them. It is a great period, and worth living for.

Conjunction, Trine, and Sextile of Uranus
This is very fortunate for artistic matters of all sorts. It brings great opportunities to artists, musicians, and actors, and all those who make their living through art in any form at all, and means the utmost development of their talents and abilities, and the opportunity to come out. In horoscopes of people who are artists, this is the transit to look for, and the first aspect by sextile, trine, or conjunction to Venus is likely to bring them to the front. The same is true in regard to literary people who have Uranus transiting Mercury. It usually brings favors, gifts, pleasure, increase of social activity, new friends, and all that makes life worthwhile from this standpoint.

Uranus in Square, Opposition, or Conjunction to Venus
This is also interesting, unconventional, and very powerful in its effect upon the emotional nature, being even more marked than the trine or sextile, and stirring up the affections to a feverish degree, causing the person to break all bonds, conventions, and ordinary limitations, and undergo a period of freedom and often an affair that may bring some notoriety or provoke Mrs. Grundy to action.

It is a time when people should try to be guided by common sense and discretion, not let their feelings get away with them, and be a little reasonable in the demonstration of their emotions. As a rule, it suddenly and unexpectedly brings someone into the life who is fascinating, clever, talented, and who aroused the love nature to the utmost, and people met under this influence are apt to go out of the life as suddenly as they came in. Under this influence, old friends disappear, die, or are separated from one, or else one runs out of patience with their old-fashioned way of doing things, their frowning and solemn respectability, and determines to go the pace. An afflicted Venus behaves very giddily, the hair curls up, the complexion blots, and the costume is posterized. Old maids take courses in osculation, exercise the eyes, and walk around the flatiron three times every windy day. Married ladies weary of the stale wedding cake and indulge in Plato, and Eleanor Glynn—Whoops my dear!

The safest course is not to take too seriously anyone who comes bounding into your aura about this time. These people will fascinate but will soon disappear, and leave the wreck behind, and woe to the maiden whose tendrils have curled around this broken reed, for the ax of the woodman will sever her twigs. Nothing satisfactory, permanent, or in any way productive of lasting happiness comes out of this aspect, and it is disruptive to the social life of the individual and all to no purpose. It leaves them with broken friendships, and old shrines deserted, and all for a passing shadow that only irritated and upset them, and gave them no real happiness. People are prone to behave rather foolishly under this aspect, and it takes a very steady Venus to withstand it. The worst of it is that it inclines people to do things that bring notoriety, criticism, and scandal, and they seem to desire to be talked about, and to aid their idiocy as thoroughly as possible.

Uranus in Evil Aspect or Conjunction to Mars
This is dangerous and indicates recklessness, want of caution and prudence, the disposition to run into danger, to take risks, and to act upon sudden and mad impulses, to do things for love of adventure, love of actual danger, and regardless of common sense. It causes people to do things they would at other times refrain from in the way of running, into experiences of the dangerous sort, taking their life in their hands, etc., if the horoscope admits of all this, and under this influence they are likely to do unusual and foolhardy things. It therefore leads to accidents and mishaps and all sorts of physical hurts. Under the aspect of Uranus square Mars in Pisces, I had a nasty accident to my foot. It stirs up the initiative,

the element of adventure, courage, and physical activity, and gives love of excitement, and may make one more aggressive and quarrelsome, and cause the temper to be quick, peculiar, and sometimes uncontrollable for the time being, when Mars is afflicted at birth.

Uranus in Favorable Aspect to Mars
These aspects bring out the more constructive side of this influence, give boldness, the ability to do reckless things without danger, and run into experiences without mishap. Where Mars is prominent and well aspected, it may bring fame or notoriety through courage, war, surgery, acts of bravery or physical recklessness and adventure.

Uranus in Evil Aspect to Jupiter or Afflicted Conjunction
This is a very treacherous influence financially, leading to risks of all sorts, speculation, games of chance, and consequent losses. At this time, one is approached by schemes and schemers, and it is dangerous to listen to them. Take no chances where money is concerned, or you will surely lose. It brings the most promising schemes and opportunities which may appear quite practical but are apt to peter out. It sometimes causes one to make large sums of money in some unusual way, and then to have it all swept away so quickly that you hardly know you have had it. Often a bank president and people who have money in trust at these times speculate with money that is not theirs and in the hope of making large winnings, but lose and are disgraced.

It is an evil time for going to lawyers, changing investments, buying or selling property, reaching out for new honors, and whatever is done in this way under this aspect nearly always turns out unfortunate. The thing to do is to be as conservative as possible in money matters, and take no chances. Uranus stirs up the ambitions and causes one to want to accomplish wonders financially, but impulses in the bad aspects are misleading and treacherous. He also sometimes stirs up the religious instincts and awakens the more humanitarian feelings, but in these aspects inclines to fanaticism, unpractical schemes, and unreliable feelings.

Uranus in Good Aspect to Jupiter
This develops the spiritual powers, adds to the desire and power to do others good, and is an inspiring influence. It broadens the sympathies and causes people to be less selfish in attitude toward mankind and generally more generous and kind. It is a spiritual aspect and in horoscopes that favor this sort of thing it is quite likely to have marked effect. But in a very subtle way. It is a delicate influence and may bring someone into the life who aids in bringing about some change for the better in the character; this may take place through books, or in some non-personal way.

Uranus in Aspect to Neptune
The transit of Uranus in aspect to Neptune works largely on the imaginative plane and does not require actual physical manifestation. Whatever does take place is likely to be very personal and perhaps very occult, and the outer world may never know it, but people will be likely to realize that some change has taken place.

Transits of the Planet Neptune

Neptune Afflicting the Moon
This aspect is likely to bring some woman into the life who either has an unfavorable influence morally or who leads one into unpractical lines of thought, manages to give one the wrong viewpoint or interests one in matters that afterwards prove misleading. Sometimes the wife or mother is affected peculiarly, and strange experiences come through them, or to them. It encourages psychic phases such as clairvoyance and trance, may give rise to some form of indulgence and is a misleading influence. The good aspects will, as a rule, bring some influence into the life that will prove to be uplifting; and expanding and during the transit one should benefit in some rather unusual or peculiar and subtle way, through some woman. The good aspect favors higher thought and meditation, a deeper understanding of the more hidden laws of the Universe and may be a means of inspiration and religious experience. All depends upon the horoscope.

Neptune Afflicting Mercury
This aspect leads to false ideas and study along impractical and unprofitable lines, and one is apt to be deceived, led astray and waste a good deal of time and thought to no purpose. It tends to medita-

tion, inactivity, desire for strange ideas and experiences, interest in uncommon books and subjects, and one may be associated with some person of strange mentality who temporarily influences one to take up ideas and lines of thought that afterward prove useless. It tends to deception, fraud, and peculiar experiences through correspondence and is a very woozy aspect. Tends in the direction of indulgence and immorality in such horoscopes, and leads the mind in the direction of dangerous ideas and practices.

The favorable aspect leads to contemplation, meditation, study in higher things, spiritualism, mysticism, etc., and one may, at this time, gain much unusual information and insight.

Neptune in Unfavorable Aspect to Venus
This leads to deceptive love affairs where one imagines he or she is in love, but really is not, or where one imagines peculiar circumstances connected with the whole affair. It is a dangerous aspect, and may associate one temporarily with someone who arouses the emotions to a very great degree. It leads to peculiar mysterious and unique experiences, and is an aspect of masquerade. Avoid having a love affair under this aspect. You will be deceived and most of it will be in the mind. This aspect tends in the direction of romance, sentiment, and has a most sensuous state that can lead in some cases to very unwise action.

Neptune in Favorable Aspect to Venus
This aspect tends to friendship and attractions of a very spiritual order, where the bond is psychic and intangible, and gives the highest order of spiritualized affection. People in one's life at this time are likely to play upon the higher nature and call out the most unselfish and impersonal side of the affections, and there will be a peculiar state of exaltation in regard to it. It often brings a very lofty refining influence.

The transits of Neptune are very subtle, working on the psychic plane, mostly and sometimes with apparently no effect, but they must be used with discretion. In horoscopes that are not at all sensitive, Neptune cannot do much, the idea being that the vibrations of Neptune are lost to sight.

Neptune in Evil Aspect to Sun, Afflicted Conjunction
A peculiar and disintegrating influence, tending to destroy the willpower, acting directly upon the psychic and emotional nature and sometimes subjecting people to strange and inexplicable lines of action the motive of which will always be the desire to sacrifice oneself for indulgence to or for others. In totally sensual and selfish horoscopes, the more the desire for indulgence of a highly exotic and emotional type. In horoscopes where the tendency is shown, they may take to drugs, indulge in fainting trance or coma, and undergo symptoms of an obscure sort.

The best sort of treatment usually is a complete change of environment and also a complete change of associates. Someone may be vampirizing the individual and it may be the one he or she is most fond of. It tends to forms of activity that are romantically alluring, dangerous either to the health or real interests, or incompatible with common sense, involving self-sacrifice, obliteration of the personality, and the submerging of oneself in some idea such as Father Damion going among the lepers.

It may bring about a temporary psychic phase and, under such cases, anaemia. It may bring temporary bad health so as to result in debility, weakness, and over-strain. The advice is to avoid the weird, romantic, exotic, and erotic, and to try to cultivate sane thoughts, keep with sane people, and be as normal as you can. This transit is likely to throw you into association with people (men) who are rather queer; do not be influenced by them. Keep the health up to par and avoid any unusual form of indulgence and you will be all right. If depleted, tired, or nervous, take a few days change of surroundings, and get right away from the people you are habitually related to, even if you do not like to do so. Vampirazation is a very common thing under this aspect. Women may have peculiar experiences with men, or their husbands, fathers, fiances, or very good friends. May either suffer from some illness or undergo unusual experiences, or there may be something extraordinary in their relations with them at this time. Whatever it is, it will be largely the work of the imagination and after it is all over they will see that they have been deceived.

Neptune in Favorable Aspect to Sun
This is entirely too subtle and purely spiritual or psychic to pay much attention to in practical notes of this sort, and you will have to watch very closely to detect its effect. It ought to be entirely on the higher altruistic plane, and ought to lead to actions and aims of a very unselfish sort, and for the time the person may have some spiritual experience, develop some psychic phase, or be actuated by some very unusually lofty sentiment that is charitable and brings unexpected benefits through inventions or untried and novel enterprises.

This is a propitious time for starting undertakings in which chance plays a part, matters connected with the governments, corporations, and in general where the interests of many people are involved. It sometimes brings money from unusual and unexpected sources, and it is a good time to invest. It is a period of gain and financial expansion, and when any opportunities of a financial sort should be looked into and taken advantage of. Opportunities that may not at first appear favorable are likely to turn out so later. It is wise to take chances under this aspect, provided there are not very strong and contradictory aspects, and it is by branching out, being unconventional, and taking a certain amount of risk that the real benefits of this aspect will appear.

Neptune Afflicting Jupiter
This aspect warns against bubble schemes, dishonesty, fraud, and people imposing on your good nature and generosity and getting money from you on false pretense. You should not allow your sympathies and feelings to sway you in a financial way. Under this

aspect, the sympathies, altruism, and higher religious feelings and emotions are called into play, and those who come in contact with you realize that you are so actuated and will be ready to take advantage of you and assist you to part with your property, which you will delight in doing under this influence. You will feel temporarily that it is your duty to be unselfish, help the helpless to be still more helpless, increase the bread line, repopulate the park benches, and put an attractive premium on idleness. If you live up to the opportunities of the aspect, you will have a mendicant waiting for you on every corner, three pious frauds on the doorstep, and several missionaries in the parlor, and when you go to church, the usher will welcome you with a fat smile. In the end your finances will have fled and you will realize the text that says, "Seek ye first the kingdom of heaven and his righteousness, and all these things shall be taken away from you."

So the thing to do is to cultivate a stern and austere appearance and when you see the wily tear-extractor heading your way, scowl like Satan, subdue your welling emotions, and close up your bowels of compassion lest they drain you dry. It is a poor policy to buy emotional exaltations from the street vendors, go to a Tristan like a decent body and get a good sound dollar's worth of dole or attend a revival meeting, have a real nice sloppy seance with a neighboring medium, or do anything but be made a bally fool of on the public streets. Take just enough change with you for carfare, one nut sundae, and a package of hairpins, and put your excess wealth in the porcelain pig on the mantle.

Neptune in Favorable Aspect
On the other hand, under the favorable aspects of the beautiful Neptune, you may safely open up and allow your feelings leeway, give your temperament an airing, and indulge in a spirituality without any fear. This aspect develops the unselfish sentiments without making a darn fool of you and leads to altruism of the sensible sort. You may have some profitable and special benefits that will come your way and that are unusual and for which you have

done nothing. I cannot be certain for I have had Neptune trine Jupiter and I do not think anything remarkable happened.

Transits

The motion of the Moon is irregular, sometimes fewer than twelve degrees per day, and sometimes more than fifteen degrees. At twelve degrees per day we have a directed method that denotes one year of life. Her motion is the same as that of the planet Saturn by transit, or, to make it plainer, say at ten days after birth, the Moon is in Taurus 10 degrees and at eleven days after birth in Taurus 22 degrees, her motion would then be twelve degrees for the fourteen hours. Hence the Moon's motion would then be twelve degrees for the twenty-four hours, which would be twelve degrees per year or the same motion, without a few minutes, as Saturn by transit.

Now, in long periods of trouble, grief, or loss, you will almost invariably find the place of the Moon by local motion, either as a conjunction, square, or opposition to Saturn by transit. That is, suppose the place of the Moon to be in Taurus, you will find that Saturn is by transit either in Taurus, Leo, Scorpio, or Aquarius, and so every good direction of the Moon is destroyed by the evil transit or excitement of Saturn and all evil aspects that they may form are excited by Saturn into action. But if the Moon be swift in motion, say fourteen or fifteen degrees per day, she will pass the transit of Saturn in two or three years, and then the unfortunate time will be over. But where you find the Moon by direction in bad aspect of Saturn by transit and the motion of the Moon about twelve degrees per day, then the man or woman will have a long spell of bad luck, and have a hard fight against fate, and if the directions be heavy or numerous it may bring about the total ruin of the native. But look to the nativity for the intensity, length, and extent of the evil that depends upon the disposition of the planets at birth.

Again, have regard to the place of Uranus by transit, for when the Moon arrives by local motion to the conjunction or opposition of that place or even the square (the former are most powerful). A most unsettled time will occur, when the mind is in constant dread of impending evil, or rather supposed evil, restlessness, and annoyances.

If the nativity shows it, the native may travel or leave his native land. The motion of Uranus by transit is only about four degrees a year and as the Moon's least motion is almost twelve degrees, this evil is not of very long continuance. This point is decided by the working of the directions.

Jupiter and Mars are very transitory, their motions being very swift at times. However, they are stationary in certain places, which may produce events of longer duration. Of this you must judge for yourself. If both planets are direct, the excitement will soon be past, and the event must soon happen. Hence sudden events both good and bad are caused by the transit of the two planets over or in aspect to the place of direction.

Periods of success may be judged by the position of the Moon and Saturn chiefly. When Saturn by transit is in sextile or trine to the place of the Moon by local motion, it is good provided the Moon does not run against Uranus. A lull in success will occur and for a certain time the native's affairs will be upside down.

The evil transit of Uranus to the Moon does not cause so much loss of money as it does perpetual worry and excitement. A dread of evil about to happen is present. If the evil is likely to operate on the private affairs, which may be learned from the nativity, the effect will be serious, leading to discord, jealously, separation, adultery, loss, or change of employment. The native will act rashly without thought or reason.

The Sun is very important in every nativity and rules chiefly the life and honor of a man. His motions is one degree per day, sometimes a minute more and sometimes a little less. His average motion per day is about one degree, which, in our method of reckoning directions, would be one degree per year. Hence, the transits of all the planets to the place of the solar directions are soon past as no planet moves at fewer than two degrees per year. Notice the periods when Saturn by transit forms the conjunction or other bad aspects of the Sun, and if a bad solar direction happens about the same time, heavy losses, ill health, loss of honor, and credit will follow—Uranus is the chief destroyer of credit. When the Sun and Uranus are in bad aspect, either by direction or transit, there being a bad solar direction to some other planet at the same time, much trouble will pour in upon the native affecting his or her honor and credit. If Saturn afflicts the Moon at the same time, much misfortune will occur and probably result in the ruin of the native.

When the Sun and Moon are both afflicted in a nativity, it is a very dangerous time for the health and welfare of the native. Death frequently occurs at such a time.

If the nativity does not show an accident, do not judge one. Let the directions be what they will. Do the same with sickness, for if the nativity be a healthy one, it will take much stronger directions to produce sickness than if it is unhealthy.

The house in which the transitory planet is placed, for instance, Saturn afflicting the Moon from the Ascendant, predisposes to a grave and melancholy state of mind, grief, and sorrow and denotes damage by the native's own acts or through errors in judgment.

If from the second house, it will affect money, property, or even liberty, and so on with the other houses, because the excitement comes from a certain house and the evil will arise by or through something ruled or signified by that house.

All the transits of planets over the places of the planets at birth or the luminaries signify nothing except when a direction occurs at the same time. But transits of planets through different houses in the same nativity are very important. Uranus transiting the Midheaven and the Moon by direct conjunction, square, or opposition produces worry and trouble in business, perpetual alarm, or affliction to native's mother. But if Uranus were in the eleventh, evil would come from friends or something ruled by that house, and the same with the other houses.

The Moon as noted moves very fast, and in many cases before she is clear on one aspect or direction, she is applying to another. This is why the positions of the planets by transit have such potent effects.

I will here mention that there are what I call unimportant nativities, or such wherein the planets are mostly cadent and in common signs. In such cases the direction must be very potent to produce any great results, and many small directions will pass without being observed.

The former will be chiefly obscure persons, such as are in the employ of others, but if you find the planets in cardinal signs and angular, then every direction that is excited to action will tell in a marked degree and produce events prominent and observable and such persons will generally be noted characters or masters and employers of men, etc.

Observe also the Moon when it is slow in motion by direction for this is not good for success and gain. The Moon slow in motion in a nativity is also unfavorable. Swift in motion signifies success, activity, and progress in general. Hence when Saturn afflicts the Moon as mentioned, and the Moon is slow in motion, it is very bad, but if the Moon is swift, the evil is not so great. If the Moon is swift, the evil is not so great. If the Moon and Saturn are of a benign nature, and she swift in motion, it is very good; but if slow, the benefit will not be so great.

Saturn rising in any nativity gives some impediment in the speech, more especially if he be in Aries, Taurus, Cancer, Leo, Scorpio, Capricorn, or Pisces. Mercury at the time in evil aspect will cause the native to stammer and he or she will be of a very nervous, suspicious temperament, and can easily be overcome by mesmerism.

By looking steadily at the native he or she will be unable to speak at all, unless with determined effort, that shakes the whole frame. If Mars should be in aspect to Saturn, it will improve the speech and there will be less stuttering, but talk will be fast and the lisp bad. It is a curious fact that persons with Saturn rising have very round tongues. That is, the end of the tongue is round and not pointed, whereas the Mercurial and lunar persons have sharp pointed tongues and can articulate very clearly and fluently. If Mercury be in Sagittarius or Pisces, or even Cancer rising and not in any aspect to Saturn, the native will be a great talker upon whose words not a shadow of dependence can be placed.

Venus and Saturn in conjunction, square, or opposition makes persons with a depraved taste and the practice of bad and unnatural habits. They are much attached to places and persons and have very keen feelings. Such persons suffer disappointment in love, sometimes committing suicide, and if Mercury be afflicted by Saturn they will be much given to shed tears and will cry and weep bitterly upon slight provocation.

www.ingramcontent.com/pod-product-compliance
Lightning Source LLC
Chambersburg PA
CBHW051711040426
42446CB00008B/823